THE FUTURE OF
CHRISTIAN
BROADCASTING
IN EUROPE

THE FUTURE OF CHRISTIAN BROADCASTING IN EUROPE

PETER ELVY

Published for
THE JERUSALEM TRUST
by **McCRIMMONS**

First published in Great Britain in 1990 by
McCRIMMON PUBLISHING COMPANY LIMITED
for THE JERUSALEM TRUST

© 1990 THE JERUSALEM TRUST

ISBN 085597 456 7

Cover design: Shuttleworth Lench Communications
Typesetting: Fleetlines Ltd., Southend-on-Sea
Lithographic artwork: McCrimmons, Great Wakering, Essex
Printed by Black Bear Press Ltd., Cambridge

Also by Peter Elvy

**BUYING TIME,
THE FOUNDATIONS OF THE ELECTRONIC CHURCH**

First published in 1986 by McCrimmons, Essex, England
Re-published as *Die gekaufte Zeit* by Wichern Verlag, Berlin 1987
Revised 1987 and re-published by XXIIIrd Publications,
Connecticut

**REPORTING RELIGION,
FACT AND FAITH**
Foreword: Martin Marty

Peter Elvy contributed the chapter:
'The Televangelists: What makes them tick?'
Published by the Polebridge Press, California 1990

To the congregation
of the Parish Church of St. Mary Magdalene,
Great Burstead, Essex

Contents

"But journalists also have to be careful about a version of the Heisenberg uncertainty principle in physics: sometimes by observing – and reporting – a phenomenon, we alter it."

Strobe Talbott, *Time* Magazine

"Evangéliser, c'est produire l'effet du Christ amplifié par les médias."

CREC-AVEX

"The act of broadcasting, however well-intentioned and sincerely executed, tears apart the unity of word and action personified in and by Jesus."

Colin Morris, writing in *Media Development*, the magazine of the World Association for Christian Communication

Foreword

by Hans-Wolfgang Hessler,

Direktor des Gemeinshaftswerks der Evangelischen Publizistik, Fernsehbeaufträgter des Rates der Evangelischen Kirche in Deutschland.

The future in Europe. In the face of current, far-reaching changes in our continent, this future promises to be an entirely different one. Borders between nations are becoming transparent, even disappearing completely. The expanding scope of media communications is altering our basic concepts of our societies. Religions, confessions and denominations can no longer ignore the new possibilities for communicating in a Europe made up of East and West. At last a revolution in thinking and in hope has a real chance in this continent. What role does the powerful and at the same time vulnerable medium of broadcasting play? What role falls to those people in broadcasting who, at whatever point they may be in the programming, try to orientate themselves towards the biblical message? Peter Elvy seeks to provide us with information on these questions – with research, analysis and vision.

Obviously Christian broadcasting is more than just the sum of all religious programmes. Commitment to this premise means co-responsibility in the broadest sense for the organisation of broadcasting, public or private. In this sense the public has always been able to expect a contribution from the Church towards a basic understanding of the mandate and function of broadcasting. They have also been able to expect that both public and private broadcasting remain clearly responsible for the concerns of society as a whole and not to particular groups; to expect that the freedom of broadcasting is always perceived as a freedom to serve and that, despite the predominance of entertainment programmes, there are also offers of counsel programmes or moments of reflection. They have been able to expect that contributions by the Churches themselves mediate the Christian message both as consolation and as irritation – in other words, a caring responsibility for mankind. Peter Elvy's inquiries confirm that there are sufficient opportunities for this.

Presence through programmes. In the course of current developments, Christian broadcasting too takes on a unique dimension. Today millions, if not the majority, of Church members experience the Church and its message via radio and television. Broadcast communication has long been an element in the service of Christian proclamation. Today's changes in Europe are creating access for many more millions of people, for whole generations, who under the pressure of political conditions had completely lost connection with the Christian tradition and the Christian community. These new possibilities confront the Churches and Christian groups with an extraordinary communal task. An undreamt-of area of trial and action presents itself.

The Christian presence which is demanded now, and will be demanded in the coming years, presupposes co-operation and partnership. This is unthinkable without a willingness and capacity for dialogue between theologians, programme-makers and audience. The on-going developments demand a new perception of the possibilities and responsibilities of the media. All should find encouragement who can live with the tensions between consensus and conflict, between identity and integration, between programme content and economic imperatives. People such as this must, at the same time, offer genuine space for the biblical message in testimony and service. Peter Elvy's comments in this regard are supportive and far-seeing.

This biblical message embraces the whole of creation. Christian broadcasting must measure up to this challenge. Peter Elvy describes this high aspiration in a forthright manner and without concessions. He exhorts the Church to see, in its involvement with broadcasting, an effective mode, an appropriate version of Church activity and life. He encourages the programme-maker not to underestimate the reality of the biblical message and its effects. He presses for a prompt departure into the future. His intervention in the cause of broadcasting as a reliable companion along the path into the future will certainly not go unnoticed.

Hans-Wolfgang Hessler

Preface

In October 1989, the Jerusalem Trust invited me to prepare a study into European religious broadcasting in a deregulated future. I was asked to present my findings to a special conference to be convened, twelve months later, at the Cranfield Conference Centre.

The book is based on more than a hundred interviews throughout Europe. In the early days of my travelling I cherished a small hope that, probably by some process of mental distillation, I might be given answers to some of the well-known problems facing Christian broadcasting. However, I soon came to the conclusion that *answers* are not the first requirement. The problem, as I see it, is that Christians in the European media are suffering from a lack of *questions*. So my purpose in this book is not to state conclusions but, like a radio interviewer, to ask *why?* and *what?*, and *how?* and thus to re-open a file that has perhaps been prematurely closed. Obviously the book is intended to serve as the background against which my presentations to the Cranfield Conference can be set. However I hope that it may also be of some interest to a wider public.

On the final pages I have included a list of names of all those communicators who have given me so much of their time and knowledge. Each of them has helped me in a significant way. I fear that inclusion in my roll of acknowledgments is but a tiny recompense for so much consideration and kindness. I am, of course, particularly grateful to the Jerusalem Trustees for their commission to undertake the preparatory work for the Cranfield Conference. Mr. Hugh de Quetteville, the Director of the Trust, and Professor Roger Baker have been unfailingly supportive. I am grateful also to the Bishop of Chelmsford for his enthusiasm for the project and for his permission to be away from his diocese for six months. The Bishop of Bradwell, as always, has given me much encouragement. Canon J.A.Kingham took the greatest possible care of my parish.

Mr. Alan Hockley, former publisher of *The Lancet*, and his wife Ann, read and corrected the typescript. Working against the clock, they improved communication in numerous ways. Mrs. Joyce Norris MBE reorganised and filed a mountain of papers and skilfully conducted my most important postal survey. As always, my wife Petra supported me constantly, from telephoning to translating, and listened patiently to too many bright ideas. My son Adrian located a great deal of material for me in London libraries. He also developed skills as a travel agent.

In a rapidly-changing situation, some of my thinking is provisional. Needless to say, nothing in this book necessarily reflects the views of the Jerusalem Trust. I record my warmest thanks to Dr. Howard Davis of the Faculty of Social Sciences of the University of Kent who, at a very busy time of year, was kind enough to read my manuscript and to suggest many improvements. Along with many distinguished people who are mentioned in this book, he cannot be held to account for its defects. Nor should he be considered to be guilty by association.

PETER ELVY

CHAPTER 1

The Study of Everything

This book is based on two journeys and, strangely, both were made at precisely the same time. One journey was intentional and carefully planned. The other seemed to happen by accident. In the first journey, I was introduced to a half-year of European radio and television. The reason behind my investigation was to take an overview of religious broadcasting; to make a mental, continental map; to feel for common threads that would be unlikely to break in Europe's deregulated future. Perhaps I should have foreseen the second – simultaneous – journey. However, I have to confess that it took me by surprise. I can best describe it as a series of accelerations in my own learning about communication. Looking back on a hundred interviews about every aspect of the electronic media, the paths of my two journeys occasionally touched. For me, the result was an almost-electric arcing: broadcasting practice sharply illuminated by communication theory.

Of course, in the long road round Europe, there have also been some perfectly tangible milestones. Careering round Tallinn in my personal taxi and meeting Estonia's emerging Christian communicators is something that I cannot forget. The invitation to Fatima to share with so many of Europe's Roman Catholic bishops in their four-yearly media conference was a privilege that I did not expect. To try to count, against the morning sunlight, the satellite dishes along Belfast's Falls Road filled me with much more than arithmetic.

But in the second, imaginary journey of ideas, I travelled further! I realised what was happening to me in my second country, Norway.

1

I was in the Danvik Folk High School at Drammen near Oslo. It is an impressive institution and specialises in media studies. At the end of the visit, one of the lecturers, Dr. Charles Peterson, an American, took me on a mountainous car ride to see the sights. Somehow, by conversational accident, I began to take Political Economy seriously. It seemed to me to be an entirely new theoretical basis for understanding the mass media. It was not quite a conversion experience but I realised that I had been shifted. Henceforth my observation of religious broadcasting must take place from a new vantage point.

And this happened again. In southern Sweden, in Malmö, an idealistic and creative television producer, Anders Lagerson, showed me that some people really believe that, in television, small can be beautiful. I had moved again. In Helsinki, Dr. Ingmar Lindqvist (an English-language guide *par excellence*) took me on a private expedition through his deeply convincing theory of communication. That day, I travelled many miles. In the great broadcasting centre of Hilversum my interview with Dave Adams, European Director of Trans World Radio, stretched from afternoon into evening. My scribbling continued over dinner. The next morning we sat down again and talked until my notebooks ran out.

In Rome, in the Salesian University (and in the nick of time) Don Franco Lever administered an antidote to Political Economy. Also I began to feel the heat of his own burning conviction that broadcasting is so much more than message transmission. A camera is not simply a neutral implement. It can provide a new (and otherwise unavailable) way of looking at reality. Once again, my ground had been shifted underneath me. Soon afterwards, in the Gregorian University, Father Robert White SJ showed me some of the signposts that point out the culturalist understanding of communication. Then, two weeks later in Portugal, Cardinal Carlo Maria Martini of Milan rose to his feet to address his fellow European bishops. With others, I was propelled towards a new conviction that the Christian Church *is* communication.

So a great part of my journeying has been happening inside my own head. The physical transportation has taken me from the USSR to Lisbon, from the Vatican to Nashville, Tennessee. For six months and more, I have thought and talked of little but

Christian communication in general and religious broadcasting in particular. No doubt it will be several years before all the momentum is expended. For the timebeing, I am left with armfuls of mental 'sketches' and very many questions. This book is, if you like, the first provisional arrangement – an album. It would be an over-confident observer who would even try to absorb and classify what is happening in twenty countries and then to portray the whole in broad, magisterial brushstrokes. This, I think, is to attempt far too much. So this book has limited objectives. The intention is not to fit all the sketches together to create a definitive panorama. There are many gaps just as there are many un-answered questions. Tentatively I offer this selection of illustra-tions. They come from my two simultaneous journeys and also, because I am me and no-one else, from my total experience of life.

But pictures, even written pictures, do not necessarily tell the truth. As the *Salesiana* would certainly remind me, the person holding the pencil or the camera can usually choose the spot on which he will stand. And this, of course, determines what the viewer will see. An objective view is a self-contradiction. We each have our own history and experience, our own interests and convictions and our own way of looking at things. Cameras, and even pencils, have an effect on the one who holds them. As Walter Ong SJ observed, they are not simply instruments but extensions and transformers of human beings. To claim *objectivity* for my observations would be to say that I have found a way of looking at life other than through my own pair of eyes – and I have not. The New Testament (very wisely!) offers no less than four gospels and several additional angles and theological perspectives. My set of pictures is but my own. If I cannot claim to be objective, I can at least try to be industrious and fair-minded, to move from place to place and (let the pictures be photographic) to select my lenses with care. Of course, like any director, I possess the awesome power of *arrangement*. I can order my material in my own way. In this process, the hope has to be for balance and insight. The ever-present dangers are distortion, over-emphasis and idiosyn-crasy.

Where will I stand first to take my first picture? This is an all-important choice and could determine the course of everything that follows. Should we begin in the world of ideas or should I try to re-create some broadcasting history? Perhaps predictably, we could go back over well-trodden ground to the very beginning of wireless. How about a view of Marconi transmitting the Morse letter S across the Atlantic from his base in Newfoundland?

On the other hand we might begin with some of the world's first religious broadcasts. The North American radio premiere was an odd, almost accidental, occasion. Anglican evensong was transmitted from Calvary Church, Pittsburg. But it was a technological rather than an ecclesiastical turning-point and it was understood as such at the time. It was the initiative of one of the choirmen, an engineer with the Westinghouse Corporation. The rector was absent.

There are so many possible beginnings. John Reith at the BBC worked out a framework and the philosophy for Britain's centralist religious broadcasting. But this is a well-observed subject, and perhaps the topic is too parochially British. Alternatively, we could begin in Rome with the once-great transmitter built by Marconi in the walled oasis behind St. Peter's. Or we could stand, as I once stood, beside *Live Aid* producer Tony Verna while the Pope (with the help of twenty-three broadcast satellites and the BIC Corporation) inaugurated the Marian Year.

From a different position in the ecclesiastical spectrum, we might focus on a missionary radio. Trans World Radio began in 1954 and now broadcasts in nearly one hundred languages. For a European beginning to this international story, we could go to Monaco, on October 16th, 1960, when a 100,000–watt short-wave transmitter at Mount Agel became available. Perhaps the greater turning point is today as TWR opens up new studios in Moscow, Kiev and Minsk. But missionary radio has had mixed fortunes in Europe. According to BBC research, Soviet listeners much prefer to listen to foreign religious broadcasts when they are part of a diverse range of programmes.

Another starting point could be the topical subject of Britain's brand-new broadcasting legislation. But this might be of no great concern to a reader in Italy, where real deregulation has long since happened. Still less would it interest Romanians, united by the Christmas heroes who seized the television station – and, six months later, re-divided by the burly miners who were called in to rough-up those in Bucharest who still complained of media manipulation.

4

There could be a long list of possible beginnings. Making a choice is not the result of some scientific process determined by objectivity. It depends upon the interests and the stance (and the constituency) of the cameraman. So, I will bring my questioning to an end and begin to reveal my own process of selection which I hope is not idiosyncratic. Incidentally it may allow me to adopt neutrality in the current hot debates about religious broadcasting and also let me avoid declaring a personal preference for Vatican Radio or Public Service Broadcasting or Trans World Radio or anyone else.

I will begin by trying to focus, not on an event in broadcasting history nor on any place in my European journeyings. I choose to begin with Communication Studies – two words that are bounced around media conferences like a ping-pong ball. And they seem, with each bounce, to acquire a brand-new meaning. What do we really think when we hear the words? What pictures come into our minds? Communication Studies. At first sight, it sounds rather like Risk Analysis or Flow Engineering – just one more new-fangled subject of doubtful civilising value.

Three thousand years ago, a beginning was made by Aristotle. In the *Rhetoric*, he described the art of persuasive speech. He suggested a three-part process: "Know your audience and their situation" (*ethos*); "Speak clearly" (*logos*); "Touch the emotions as well as the mind of your listener" (*pathos*). Not too many years ago, both faith and politics were both built on rhetoric. The great debates between Abraham Lincoln and William O. Douglas owed everything to oratory and nothing to image making. In Downing Street, Harold Macmillan was the last rhetorician, just as he was certainly the first prime minister to understand television. In public life, rhetoric is now only a memory and the very word has suffered a change of meaning. However the ancient art of persuasive speech still survives and flourishes in the modern advertising industry.

As the Western world entered into a new age of mass media, latter-day Aristotles began to put forward new and different theories of communication. One was born, in the 1940s, in a North American engineering laboratory. A few years later, a totally different way of thinking – as different as chalk from cheese – began to emerge in post-war Europe, with an emphasis on meaning rather than message. In more recent years a successor group has begun to look not just at communication but at culture which is communication's result.

Engineers, psychologists, students of linguistics and many, many more have been involved. On the whole, the Churches have not been engaged. Churchmen have been keen to be involved in the mass media but they have been less interested in thinking about the meaning of this activity. Like so many motorists, they would rather not know what is going on under the bonnet. Communications Studies hardly features in theological education and, when it does, it is reduced to hands on experience – a brief introduction to the hardware.

"On the other hand, Communication Studies might be just the thing for Felicity – especially if one day she wants to get a job in television. After all, communication is the thing of the future, isn't it?"

But can human communication be studied as a unity? *Felicity's* perfume, *his* rude sign from the back of a taxi, *that* graffiti-smothered train, *these* gas bills – can they all be lumped together within one sagging pair of academic brackets? Is Communication Studies an appropriate name? Is there one box of intellectual tools that can be used to unpick a smile on a human face and then go to work on an advertisement on the side of an office block? How can a lingering kiss on a railway platform belong with the train timetable? Why not offer a university degree in the Study of Everything? And, come to think of it, didn't the Chinese do just that? Didn't the budding civil servant sit down in a little hut for three weeks and write down everything he knew about about everything? Or is that just another Mandarin tall story?

Communication is everything there is in life – or just about everything. Without communication, there could be no relationship, no culture, no civilisation, no sex, no language, no anything. Why do we cry so hard for Terry Waite or Helen Keller or the Man in the Iron Mask? Is it not because there is no greater horror than to retain consciousness but to be deprived of communication; to be held in close confinement, *incommunicado*? To the salesman or the preacher, communication is a another word for persuasion. Rather nearer to heaven, the poet meditates, but includes you and me. Communication is God's greatest gift to the human family. And the real key to the Christian scriptures is the magnificent insight that, finally, when the family suffered a communication breakdown, the word became flesh.

But does all communication ride on invisible rails? Can we hope to speak of a science? Can we assume the existence of yet-to-be-uncovered laws explaining one ecosystem of communication? Or should we retreat down the road into that other building marked Humanities?

Things are quite different when we consider something like climatology. Now there's a subject as wide as any ocean! It deals with matters so convoluted and multifarious and unpredictable that there isn't a computer alive that could answer a straightforward question about the warming of the Atlantic. But, wildly ambitious though they are, climatologists are at least reasonable. We can take their endeavour into our minds. We know what they want to do and our best guess is that, one day, they (or their grandchildren) will get close to achieving it. But communication is an ocean of oceans. And, in every direction, the boundaries are so far over the horizon that they cannot be delineated.

But there it sits in the undergraduate prospectus: *"Communication Studies (BA or BSc), a three-year introduction to Everything"*.

Meanwhile, in the Church (which for centuries has been the accepted repository of all serious knowledge about Everything), it seems that Communication Studies might never have been born. Of course, like any big institution, the Church likes to take its time when it comes to new ideas. Many years have to elapse before things filter through. It takes decades for young midshipmen to become admirals with authority for action. But one place where we might reasonably expect to see early results is in those schools of navigation where the midshipmen are trained.

Take for example the British case of Henry Tudor College. It's a fairly typical seminary for the preparation of the Church's full-timers. The students come from many backgrounds and nowadays even Felicity could be granted observer status. In these friendlier times, it might be best not to enquire too much about Henry Tudor himself. Whether he was the Catholic Seventh or the anti-Roman Eighth or even a Welsh Baptist hymn-writer can be left as one of life's unanswered questions. The Dean (his two immediate predecessors went higher) lives in a permanent state of siege. When he is not worrying about numbers, he is preoccupied with staffing, buildings or his place in the league table. Then he has to attend to the forests of paper unheedingly recycled by his communicating superiors.

Daily he is assailed by reminders that he should take account of this and that. Like Thomas Cranmer before him, he is blown about by every wind of doctrine that comes from headquarters. But, manager that he is, nearly everything gets squeezed in somehow. Time is found to introduce his students to the world; evenings with youth projects, weeks in the inner city or in bottling plants and talks on marriage counselling. Very reasonably, the midshipmen imbibe a special concoction of many tastes.

And could a small corner be found for communication? "Quite impossible," comes an impatient sigh from Henry Tudor College. But others do manage to squeeze in an afternoon for a visit to a local radio. But mostly, even when a tiny space is found – far from even glancing in the direction of Everything – all that is provided is an hour or two for the more adventurous midshipmen to play creatively with a camera or a tape-recorder. And this is by no means only a British condition. Often it is the theological colleges that are sited furthest away from their European and American roots who are more prepared to look in new directions. One Geneva-based communications director utters a sad lament: "They don't worry much in Tübingen about the Lutheran World Federation but they do in Arusha".

The problem is immense. Almost anything, large or small, ridiculous or sublime, can be investigated under the umbrella of Communication Studies. Everything is there somewhere: Typing lessons, nuclear war, Yves St. Laurent, liberation theology, Saatchi and Saatchi, cultural studies, video technique, screen studies, personal relations, voice projection or readings in St. John's Gospel. This really has to be the study of Everything and, of course, the only safe way to cope with that is either to ignore it or diminish it until it becomes that something you want it to be, confined to half an hour on a Friday afternoon.

We are left with awkward conclusions. Communication is clearly Everything. But coherent Communication Studies seems to be a mission impossible. It is not a science but a field of interest, leaving everyone free to make an individual set of definitions. Nevertheless Henry Tudor College should do more. Half a day with a tape recorder is at least something; a sacramental nod to that great science-in-the-sky in which we would probably like to believe but which cannot be said, with certainty, to exist.

The alternative, the dream, is certainly amazing. If, one day, Communication Studies turns out to be true, half an hour on a Friday afternoon will assuredly not be enough. Our thinking will be revolutionised. The time for options and extras will be past. We will no longer be gazing into a cathode ray tube, darkly. Far from being a new-fangled satellite interest, Communication Studies would inherit the earth. We would no longer think about a component. We would be in a new dimension.

As for the Churches, our structures, our special efforts in evangelisation, our scriptures – even our theology – would have to be looked at through an entirely new set of lenses. This is a thought too worrying to contemplate and it may explain why most branches of theology have kept a safe distance from anything calling itself Communication Studies. The quest for this Holy Grail has been left to the engineer, the political economist, the audience measurer, the sociologist and many others. And because the challenge seems so overwhelming, each specialist has looked down from his own tower and each has arrived at his own set of meanings. Where theologians have enlisted, they have usually chosen to wear the borrowed colours of other disciplines.

However, there have been clear distinctions between the Communications Studies of North America, the Third World and Europe. In the United States, the cause of scholarship was given something of a fillip by the *coup d'etat* which allowed the Electronic Churchmen to displace their Mainline cousins. Liberal Christians became considerably more interested in Communications Studies because it gave them a opportunity to investigate those who had supplanted them. Could this mean that, when religious communicators are left with time on their hands, they develop a greater interest in theorising? Could it also mean that Communication Studies as a theoretical activity has evolved through too close an association with professional communicators?

CHAPTER 2
Communication theories

My second picture is a personal memory. Many years ago, in 1947, when I was quite a small boy, I spent most of my time with a special friend. Our war-surplus world was still full of gas masks and ammunition boxes. On the ground behind our houses we fought epic battles. Potato pistols spat in all directions and water bombs rained down. Every now and then, we would retire to our headquarters, a lookout cunningly constructed right in the middle of a thick hedge and with a false front made of camouflaged wire mesh. Communication would hardly have satisfied Rommel. For our top-secret messages, we relied on a technique known to millions of small children; cocoa tins connected by a long length of taut string. Most messages probably consisted of 'Can you hear me?' which ought not to surprise any serious student of communication.

Four years before, two American scientists, C. Shannon and W. Weaver were engaged in rather similar experiments in the laboratories of the Bell Telephone Company. It is inconceivable that these two scientists saw themselves as Fathers of Communications Studies but (like the Saints) that is what, in retrospect, we have made them. Almost in the terms of my childhood games, Shannon and Weaver tried to measure how much information can be meaningfully transmitted from A to B. Their work was part of the war effort with an obvious military spin-off.

Their communications model could hardly be more straightforward. They thought in terms of messages. Each message needs to

10

be encoded, transmitted, decoded and received. This, after all, is how a telephone seems to operate. There are two remaining questions: How much information can be made to travel along this communication pipeline? To what degree is the meaning of the message diminished by communication defects and distractions? Shannon and Weaver called these problems 'noise', just as we talk about a disturbing crackle on a telephone line or 'snow' on a TV set.

Published in 1949, Shannon and Weaver's *Mathematical Theory of Communication* remains important. Down the years, other theorists have devised variations. But the idea of a sender transmitting a message seems to fit many of the facts. When A has something to say to B, the task is for that something to be transmitted in such a way that,like the box of chocolates, it will arrive undamaged in the same state of freshness in which it left the manufacturer.

Needless to say, the concept of message transmission fits easily into into our information-hungry culture. The advertising industry has been built on message transmission. Mass media ('A-to-B x millions') means that one message can blanket a whole population. And this is not something that many of us resist. Most of us spend a good part of our disposable income improving our personal reception facilities. The letter box is as old as the house but now we have added to it a telephone system, several radios, almost certainly, a television or two and, perhaps, a satellite receiver or a cable terminal.

When it comes to the electronic mass media, we spend most of our lives as Bs. We are receivers of messages and we structure our lives and arrange our furniture for optimum reception. We are told we live in an age of mass communication but this is untrue. Ours is an era of mass information, mass entertainment and mass production of the same messages. As far as the electronic mass media are concerned, the message goes down a one-way street. And that is only half the story. Entertainment broadcasting is only part of the growing worldwide network of electronic message-sending. Day and night, streams of data flow from every corner of the planet from hundreds of millions of sources. And the traffic is doubling and redoubling.

The application of the A-to-B concept to preaching may seem too obvious to mention. But here, depending on your religious point of view, we have an interesting example of the ultimate inadequacy of the Shannon and Weaver theory. Is the Christian gospel a message in the technical sense of the word? Does the gospel have a reality that is independent of its sender? Is the gospel self-evident information? Can the gospel be received in the same condition in which it was sent? Is 'noise' the only reception problem?

Of course the so-called Televangelist might reply that, for electronic preachers, there are special arrangements and the Holy Spirit is always available as a special aid to clear reception. This is certainly a refinement of the Shannon and Weaver model. Of course, we claim that the gospel is good news. ('News' might seem to seem to be assured of a comfortable place in a telephone laboratory.) But is the gospel a message in the Shannon and Weaver sense? Is it information waiting for a carrier? Even if it is, do all messages suit all media?

The Process School (Shannon and Weaver by another name) is one useful way of looking at communication but it is not a key that will open every door. It is not a multi-purpose tool for all communication analysis. It is one specialised implement that does one specific thing, rather like a fishing line that has been baited and weighted for one species of fish. The idea of communication-as-a-process fits some situations but not others. Often in life (much more often than not!) B receives a message that has *not* been sent by A and this is not simply caused by inadequate reception or intrusive noise. We use expressions like 'getting hold of the wrong end of the stick' or 'crossed wires' and that is the process going wrong. But something far more significant is the human character-istic of seeing what we want to see, or hearing what our culture or class makes us hear.

Some of the clearest examples are religious. The Rastafarian faith depends on the role of the Haile Selassie of Ethiopia. We can be sure of few things in life but one of them is that the emperor was a Coptic Christian and did not seek to be a West Indian messiah. But he was! Many observers draw attention to a phenomenon which can be observed within many cultures. For instance, when an anti-American audience watches a cops and robbers epic, the cheering and applause come in the wrong places – on the occasions when the police get a drubbing and the robbers escape. But why stop with anti-Americans? How do you react when a huge motorbike roars up to your house and a young man with lank hair, covered in leathers from head to toe and his chest adorned with brass studs, knocks politely on your door?

Examples can be misleading if they fail to emphasise that our creation of meaning is a constant process. We continually react and re-react to our environment and our history. Whether there is a message or not, we create our own meanings for everything. The analysis of this interrelated web of reactions is called semiotics or semiology. Literally, it means the study of signs. Semioticians are less interested in messages and far more interested in the system of relationships between signs that we find in our surroundings.

To the semiotician, there is no *wrong* reading of a message. Meanings are not determined by *content* but by the structural properties of the sign system. Your meaning is the meaning that matters and that is where we must start. The local cleric may think that the most important thing in his church is the cross on his altar, the bible on his lectern or the font for his babies. But the people who live near the church may see things entirely differently. Perhaps the thing they value most is the pleasing *exterior* of the building ('the look of the place'). Perhaps they value the charming gilded weathercock because, when he was blown off in a gale, the whole community willingly paid up to have him re-instated. Now the clergyman's personal reaction to this may be one of horror, disappointment or determination to ram home his theological certitudes in a leaflet drop. But all that won't alter the present facts, the meanings of the moment. And the communicating pastor is the one who is in touch with his neighbours' reality; who can first understand and then work within their meaning system.

So where did semiotics come from? If history ran on rails, there would have been a second telephone laboratory and, as soon as it became apparent that Shannon and Weaver had not quite given a definitive answer to the meaning of life, two fresh engineers would have put their heads together and, with hardly a thought for the Nobel Prize, promptly tidied up the tiresome inconsistencies that continually crop up in Area B – meanings unconnected to messages.

Just about everything else has happened in semiotics but not that. Most of the action has been in Europe and there has not been an engineer in sight. In fact, the history of the study of semiotics is completely unrelated to anything achieved by Shannon and Weaver. The 'Process School' and 'Semiology' stand side-by-side as chapter headings in the text books but that is because we can look in two directions and see them coming. But each has little interest in the other. They are as different as plumbing and psychiatry. However, both use the *code* concept and they both seek to comprehend *structures* of communication. In the case of semiotics, this is the *structure of signification.*

Semiotics is hardly a well-fenced academic paddock. It is more a state of mind. There have been many parents and many separate births. If we look back at the way people have been thinking about signs and meanings, we see that the story is a complicated flow chart – something like an Underground railway map. Some lines come together. Other passengers travel right through the central area, shooting under all the other lines. Loosely-related streams of thinking can all be called semiotics. But no-one has ever woken up in the morning, pinched herself and exclaimed: "I'm a semiotician, by gosh I am".

Realism, first in the novel and later in cinema, is a major source. But have we left Communication Studies for Psychology? Why do our eyes fill with tears as the hero mounts the gallows or the little heroine finds her destiny? We know that we are in a cinema and the chocolate bar is melting in our hands. Part of our brain knows where we are. In five minutes, we will be outside again in the evening bustle. But still we are crying, making an emotional response to a text – a tale well told.

On the whole, the slow tears and the sweaty palms occur within an embarrassed adult darkness. These are not easily shared experiences. But they did not always happen in the shade. When we were small children, our media-induced para-social behaviour was far less inhibited. Many a small boy, complete with cowboy hat and with his pants at half-mast, has sat on his potty in front of the family television and hollered and fired back at the bad guys on the screen. And all this raises a mighty question for those of us who aspire to be grown-up. The televised news of a real-life tragedy can upset us but a filmed fiction can produce a far bigger lump in our throat. What does that say about the way meaning is created by the mass media?

In the decade of Gorbachev and Yeltsin, Marxism may seem rather antique. But, Neo-Marxism is by no means sinking with the mother ship and remains a potent source in semiotic analysis. In the 1940s, the great questions for the Neo-Marxists was "Why haven't the workers risen up to overthrow their oppressors? What has gone wrong with the prediction that in the end the proletariat will sit in the driving seat?"

Their answer was that people are still held down by repressive institutions, and included among these are the mass media. We are bought off by the trinkets of capitalism's degraded culture industry. We are fed with news and entertainment that brainwashes us with a bourgeois value system. Instead of Hitler's storm-troopers, consumerist advertisements now leer down on the masses. What we think we are getting is *television* but what, in fact, we are getting is a *product*, provided by capitalists to control us and increase their capital. So the media are instruments of oppression, means of regimenting the ordinary people and imposing social control.

This was the thinking of the Frankfurt School and its keystone work, Theodor Adorno's and Max Horkheimer's *Dialectic of Enlightenment*. The echoes of Frankfurt can be heard everywhere in Communication Studies. Liberation theology draws heavily on the Frankfurt worldview. In the global village, class oppression is now also understood as North-South oppression. The mass medium is the obvious weapon, far more subtle than imperialism. Culture and language are threatened. Most of the world is held in thrall to a new economic colonialism. And all the while, a wily media temptress, from her lair deep in the North Atlantic, positions her squadrons of satellites. She sings her victims into a trance that leaves them brain-damaged, awake to nothing but consumerist cravings and an artificially implanted vision of the world.

But some are content to make value judgments about the *content* of television. The presumption is that TV can be either good or bad, wholesome or dangerous, uplifting or pornographic. Like the internal combustion engine or nuclear power or any technological advance, television can be used for good or ill. A motor car can either run a sick child to hospital or it can be used in a terrorist raid. Everything depends on the intention of the user. The gadget itself is morally neutral. But is everything as simple as that? Motor cars have a cumulative, ecological effect. Millions of ambulances pollute the atmosphere just as severely as millions of getaway cars.

And the same applies to television. Is it a parallel to cigarette smoking? Should each TV set carry a government health warning? Regardless of the quality of the programmes, there may well be a long-term, cumulative effect on our perception of reality.

The study of culture is yet another way into an understanding of communication. It was Bonhoeffer who saw that the way to understand a culture is to analyse its communication. If culture is "all that man has added to nature", it has been communication (primarily language) that has made this addition possible. Indeed, there could be no culture without communication. *Homo incommunio* could have added nothing. So, for instance, when the insights of cultural studies are applied to the North American Televangelists, each is understood as a *symbol* of a cultural and social reality. Televangelist Robert Schuller is the representative token of a particular, and under-represented, socio-religious class. When he goes (if his class still exists) another symbolic figure will fill his ecological niche. Thirty-five years before Schuller, Archbishop Fulton Sheen filled a particular media vacuum. However, a reincarnation of Sheen is no longer possible. Nowadays his brand of American Catholic churchmanship does not exist.

There are many shades of opinion but Communications Studies itself seems to have been seduced by the power and pervasiveness of television. Other media are neglected. The interrelation between television and other media is too often ignored. Much that passes for Communication Studies is in fact Television Studies and concentrates entirely on the special power of television to influence attitudes and distort reality. The ways of understanding mass communication are legion. By no means all are negative. One of the oldest, Stephenson's neglected play theory of communication, sees a therapeutic value in mass entertainment – a chance to laugh at the boss and the policeman in a way that is not possible in real life. But many communications theorists (too many!) have abandoned the search for good television. Instead, they understand the medium in terms of its overall effect. And also there is a hugely influential group of investigators who try to enter into Televisionland to make a census of its electronic inhabitants.

The majority of the characters in this Televisionland are young adult whites. The men are sexually successful and violent. There are no lavatories or nasty smells. Hair never needs combing and venereal disease does not exist. The married men are usually dull fellows. The women are much-divorced and have violence done to them. God has died in this cathodic country. But the problem with Televisionland is not only its glossy inhabitants. The problem is television itself and its inbuilt propensity to distort. Sadly, nothing is sacred, not even the news. When they published *Bad News*, *More Bad News* and *Really Bad News*, Glasgow University's Media Group pointed out the ways in which the cumulative effect of news stories is to maintain the social *status quo*. The group's findings were not popular. Lord Annan described the members as a "shadowy guerilla force on the fringe of broadcasting".

Nowadays lack of faith in the total truthfulness of television is hardly revolutionary and our depression becomes acute when the audience figures are thrown into the pot. Television is not watched by the programme but by the clock. Professor George Gerbner of the University of Pennsylvania tells us most of what we need know about the statistics: "More than one half of our (American) homes turn it on in the morning and turn it off at night". The problem is television's overwhelming volume, coupled with well-founded doubts about its effects. Gerbner hits another nail on the head: "Most of the stories, told to most of the children... are told not by the parents, not by the schools, not by the Church, but by a small group of distant corporations." There is a growing awareness that the media market is not all it seems. The world's newsstands appear to be bulging with choices. Television channels are multiplying. But beneath this show of variety, there is another process. The world's mass media are being concentrated into the hands of a dozen super corporations. The heirs of Frankfurt will say 'I told you so'. But the concern about the power of the media oligopoly is worldwide. It is shared by politicians of every stripe and it interests every school of Communications Studies. Never before in human history have so few possessed so much media power over so many. Will this lead to the homogenisation of the world's culture as well as its commerce?

So, where do our disparate Communications Studies take us? Faced with the growing (some would say malign) power of the mass media, Communication Studies has taken on a personalised emergency role. In a world where human perceptions are being threatened by television, what is needed is media awareness. In *Travels in Hyper Reality*, Umberto Eco speaks of the need for a resistance force of "semiotic guerillas". Marshall McLuhan advocated "civil defence from media fallout". It may be a losing battle. But the negative aspects of the mass media must not be pushed too hard. It can be argued that the mass media have made the world a slightly safer place – from 'big bangs', at least. Television has played a major part in raising the Iron Curtain. On a planet facing ecological disaster, television may have arrived just in time. It may yet prove to be our most effective alarm bell. In any case, television is not going to go away. Something like it will remain till the end of time and it may be over-optimistic to hope for media redemption. "Stop the world, I want to get off" is profoundly disabling and leads nowhere. It is also an unChristian reaction. The attitude of this book is that it would be naive to expect perfection, or even moral neutrality, in the mass media. It is equally foolish to pretend that we live in a world in which the mass media do not exist. We live in a compromised and complicated world but it is precisely the same world that God so loved. And in any case, just for the moment, we have nowhere else to go.

A Christian television strategy cannot be built on anything but involvement. Like any incarnation, this will always involve insecurity and great risk. The problem with most of the schools in Communication Studies is that they do not take us very far along the road towards involvement. Each one looks from afar through its own, highly specialised lens. A wide-angle view is the only way of understanding such an all-pervasive medium. Television has to be handled, warts and all. It needs to be understood as something that Robert White SJ and others call a polysemy in which different levels of discourse can take place *simultaneously*. So the undoubted danger of television does not have to be its whole story. Of course, we will find distortion, exploitation and cultural imperialism. But that is not all we need discover. At the same time, some will be looking into their screen for solace. Others may even be finding 'fiesta'. Later in this book (Chapter 7) a number of Christian communicators will give a personal account of how their own Communications Studies brings them to an understanding of television. In the meantime, we will turn to the collective attitudes of the European Churches.

CHAPTER 3

Christian attitudes to broadcasting

"La radio et la télévision sont aussi des pseudo-sacrements de la présence, une 'téléprésence réelle'. Un des slogans de Radio Télé Luxembourg n'était-il pas: 'Jamais seul avec RTL!' Par la prière, devant le Saint Sacrement, nous parlons á Dieu et il nous écoute en silence. La radio ou la télé nous parlent continuellement sans nous écouter. Elles ne peuvent que nous offrir l'illusion d'une présence."

Guy Martinot SJ [1]

The Christians of Europe have been much more interested in using the techniques of broadcasting than in asking questions. What would happen if religious programming simply came to an end? Nothing, according to Monsignor Francesco Ceriotti, director of Social Communications for the Italian Bishops' Conference. "Television is just a support. The Catholic Church does not have an indispensible reliance on broadcasting." Says Dr. Rune Larsen, the Swedish broadcasting historian: "We produce many religious programmes. Perhaps their function is to show that the churches are alive in society." But is there any justification for religious broadcasting other than for showing that Christianity is still alive? Are religious broadcasts intended to achieve anything? It has been said that they soften the hard ground for the local church. Perhaps they nourish a folk culture which, although not churchgoing, is in some sense Christian – or, at least, religious.

British broadcasters point to the very healthy viewing figures for the peak-time *Songs of Praise*. It has a bigger audience than BBC

Radio's perennially popular *Woman's Hour*. Should the British churches be encouraged? Does the *Songs of Praise* audience prove that there is a religious groundswell? Perhaps one last heave by a local clergymen will pull some of these viewers into St. George's. Viewing figures follow a broadly predictable pattern. *Songs of Praise* has a good audience because it is broadcast between 6.40 pm and 7.15 pm on Sunday evenings. It sits between two popular programmes. But a TV audience can be unfaithful. How many viewers would follow the programme to a new slot at 11.30 pm? On the other hand, the audience reaction must go some way towards justifying the programme's prime position. Or does it keeps its place because a somewhat similar programme appears on the opposing channel?

Of course, the assumption is that *Songs of Praise* is a religious programme. But, what if viewers do not watch the programme for religious reasons? Administratively, of course, the programme is part of a religious broadcasting department. But a better way of categorising programmes is to look at the reaction of the receiver and not simply at the intentions of the sender or the gatekeeper. We also need the services of sociologists of religion. Audience measurers tell us too little. We need to know *why* people watch television. In the words of one communication researcher, Harry Hiller, "We need a clearer picture of what becoming a viewer means to a viewer". In 1985, two other researchers, Gaddy and Pritchard, began to test the interesting hypothesis that worship in church and worship on the TV screen are functionally similar but that one of them is of course far less burdensome. As people like their burdens to be as light as possible, why are the churches not emptier?

Professor Thorleif Pettersson of Uppsala University is among those who have followed up this *uses and gratification* communication theory in broadcast worship. [2] His conclusion, based on postal surveys involving up to 4,600 viewers, is that church worship and TV worship do indeed provide similar levels of gratification. However, only in the case of the S socio-economic group is the type of gratification, and therefore the function, the same. For every other group, the gratifications obtained by sitting in a pew and sitting in front of a TV screen are different. In other words any programme content can serve practically any purpose. So, most of those people who are gratified by TV worship services are gratified in no different way than when they watch football or a game-show. Pettersson's conclusion is that people who watch and enjoy televised worship do not do so for particularly *religious* reasons. They tune in simply because they like the programme. So high viewing figures tell us very little about a nation's folk religion. Indeed folk religion itself is probably a meaningless term.

The same question is approached but from a statistical angle in *Godwatching*, a short background book for the British IBA's consultation on 'Religious Broadcasting in the 1990s'. It seems that religious programmes are as popular to the audience as comparable programmes with the same availability. Most people do not watch at a regular time. But over a period, most television watchers occasionally see a religious programme. The IBA research (based on large-scale surveys carried out in 1986/7 and a repeated investigation in 1988) concludes that the religious broadcasting on Britain's public-service channels is not, as is so commonly-supposed, a ghetto. It stands with programming often considered to be mainstream television. However, the traditional religious programme does not seem to be doing much to help viewers cope with their personal problems. The most helpful programmes are documentaries showing real life situations. Discussion programmes by clergymen, hymn singing and church services are the least helpful. Why then does hymn-singing often occupy a prominent prime-time slot? Because it justifies itself in televisual rather than religious terms. We may think of hymn-singing as religious television. Other consumers may receive it as something else.

This may disappoint some Protestants and Catholics who have had to overcome early misgivings about sharing their worship with a wider public. Does anything happen when a parish mass appears in a Glasgow front room? One result may be entirely positive. There is a great deal of anecdotal evidence that in divided and prejudiced communities, television is the only window into the opposing camp. Comments like: 'That's the only time I've ever seen Protestant services' have got to be a great deal better than nothing. But questions about the *religious* effect of broadcast worship are difficult to answer. No doubt, the worshippers in front of the camera feel encouraged and the clergy feel on top of the world. But are the viewers converted? Does television simply reinforce attitudes? Does it ever change them? Both Thorlief Pettersson and the IBA researchers emphasise the point that the television public sees religious programmes as being mainly for others. "What a splendid programme for the heathen", thinks the churchgoing family as they watch the Sunday service. "What a splendid programme for the believer", replies the football-loving heathen, just before he switches channels. "Chewing gum for the eyes", thinks the religious sophisticate who does not like television anyway.

Some would say that, apart from waving the ecclesiastical flag, religious broadcasting is not particularly significant. But try telling that to the Ukrainian who tuned in to Vatican Radio for forty years or the one-in-five men in Kenya's towns who in 1972 were regular listeners to Radio Voice of the Gospel. Broadcasting historians will surely find that radio has had a far greater evangelistic effect than television. What is certain is that the overall religious impact of television owes very little to its religious programmes. Radio religion may have helped the faith of some of us but television, with or without its religious programmes, has so changed all our lives that it has changed religion. George Gerbner and many others now argue that television has in several ways *replaced* the church. The broadcasting industry has taken over most of the culturally-formative roles of Christianity. The value system and worldview of most of the population is determined, not by theology, but by television. So what is now left for the preacher or for the newspaper proprietor?

Faith, in the New Testament Church, was brought about by hearing the word. "Is faith still possible for those whose psyche has been predominantly formed by the image industry?" asks the Jesuit writer Avery Dulles. But others are more sanguine. In the Italian Catholic Church, there is a determination to work with television, to train parishioners to live with it, to understand it and not to see it as an adversary. TV cannot be blamed for everything. The Italian Church detected a marked decline in church attendance "long before the explosion of the mass media". But the questions remain. Why engage in religious broadcasting? Can religious broadcasting achieve anything that is religious, or even real?

Seventy years ago, the European churches were still powerful and proud. The tide of Christendom had not fully ebbed. The first reaction of churchmen to broadcasting was that it made no essential difference. Obviously the wireless was a marvel. It could shrink numbers and distance. It could allow unlimited numbers to eavesdrop on situations where previously only two or three had been gathered together. But broadcasting did not *change* things. A church service and a radio service were essentially the same. So it would be improper to broadcast services on Sundays at a time when they would compete with traditional churchgoing. On the other hand, the Churches wanted their own place on the airwaves because they wished to stake their claim in the history and culture of their communities.

Curiously there has been a double result. As well as giving a welcome re-exposure to the major religious traditions, broadcasting has also enforced a certain parity among the once-competing churches and with other institutions. Now in the 1990s, as the century closes, the churches, once the embodiment of so many European nation states, are less important. They are components in a wider community. For decades the obstacles to social pluralism have been erected, no longer by the church, but by political systems. Now that the empires of Hitler and Stalin have fallen, almost all the states of Europe appear to be on converging paths. A degree of equality between various Christians is taken for granted. This is a new phenomenon but the history of the Netherlands provides an interesting exception. Several centuries ago, the pre-ecumenical Dutch prudently concluded that those who do not hang together may well hang separately. From the beginning, an interdenominational balance has been built into their broadcasting.

In Britain, the Anglican Church played the prominent part in launching religious broadcasting. BBC religion was characterised by an unspecific 'manly' Protestantism. It was an article of faith that religious controversy be avoided at all costs. Initially British Roman Catholics were uneasy about such a centralist broadcasting philosophy. Seventy years on, Catholics have swung happily into line with the national Establishment. They are among the strongest defenders of the the public-service ideal. Nowadays, it is the much-multiplied Evangelicals who express the keenest dissatisfaction. In the Federal Republic of Germany they feel even more excluded. Access to state broadcasting is largely in the hands of the the two historic churches: the Lutherans (also called Evangelicals) and the Catholics. Centuries ago, after the Thirty Years War,

Germans learned about religious co-existence. A Catholic-Protestant duopoly evolved and is reflected in modern broadcasting. Both churches are handsomely supported from public taxes. In German religious broadcasting, 'Two's company, three would definitely be a crowd'.

In the 1920s, the North European Churches willingly grasped the opportunity to play a part in national broadcasting. They began by organising their own services, from churches of their own choice. For years, London's St. Martin-in-the-Fields served as a kind of national church-of-the-air and it had its counterparts in many European capitals. In many countries, the majority Churches took the initiative. Many still occupy the high ground. To this day, broadcast worship is fully organised by the Finnish Lutheran Church rather than by the national broadcasting company. The Church acts as agent for the minority denominations who say they are well satisfied with the arrangement. In the South of Europe, in a very different political and religious environment, another system evolved. More than fifty years ago, *Rádio Renascença* was born in Portugal. It is still a wholly-owned subsidiary of the Portuguese Catholic Church. *Rádio Renascença* is highly successful, with many more listeners than either the national or local radio services. Now it has been offered a preferential place in Portugal's new commercial television.

In the beginning religious programmes were a hugely important part of wireless output. It is probably unwise to read too much into the reasons behind this high volume of material. Perhaps religion, like music, was a ready-made audio-source. Perhaps the Church was noisily available – waiting to fill the air. In Sweden no less than twenty per cent of all the early wireless output was religious. But then came a shift and in the 1930s, many wings were clipped. In the totalitarian states, broadcasting became a valuable new weapon of government control. In the democracies, the nature of each national radio monopoly was clarified. The Churches were not evicted from the airwaves. Far from it. But they had to submit themselves to new professionals. Religious programmes were now in the hands of producers who were sympathetic but who owed their primary loyalty to the broadcasting corporations.

After the carnage of the First World War, the Church never regained its lost ground nor its credibility. Perhaps the Twenties were a frivolous dream. Europe, like America, was destined to come down to earth with a crash, to unemployment and economic depression. In the Thirties, reality caught up with life, just at the very time when public broadcasting gained confidence and self-definition. The Church's cover was blown. The ecclesiastical fairy tale was finally over. In the North European democracies, at least, if churchmen wanted to keep their place in the new public-service broadcasting, they could not simply march into the studio on their own triumphalist terms. Broadcasting would be a showcase of national news and culture. Religion would be given the place it deserved – and perhaps a little bit more than it deserved. But henceforth, religion on the wireless would not be given an absolutely free run. Alongside there would be programmes *about* religion. Gradually even humanists were invited to argue their case to representative churchmen, while cultivated neutrals held the middle ground. Pluralism had arrived. In the BBC at least, it would grow stronger until the temporary re-marriage of nationalism and religion during the Second World War.

So almost from the beginning of wireless, the Churches had to adapt to the new medium. In Britain there was little conflict. On many occasions, Archbishops Davidson and Lang expressed their pleasure at the way things were going at the BBC. Anglican worship was basking in an uncontroversial, and new, national exposure. The bishops were strongly positioned in the Sunday Committee (later the Churches Radio Advisory Committee). Of course the Church could not take broadcasting initiatives. It lacked the authority, capacity and interest to do so. It did, however, possess – and use – a considerable ability to restrain and criticise. Sunday radio was a particular preoccupation. Sunday was kept special – and dull – until the beginning of the Second World War. Then the Nazis put a stop to Radio Luxembourg. At a stroke they rebuilt the BBC's declining Sunday audiences. To the Church of England, an institution of very great influence but with only a minor media tradition, the role of watchdog seemed to be all that was required.

The view from Rome was very different. On the whole, the Catholic Church was fearful of the mass media. The risk of infection from secularism and socialism seemed too great. Some of the direst warnings were contained in Pius XI's encyclical *Vigilante Cura*. When the wireless era opened, the Italian Church owned twenty daily newspapers. The Church's involvement in broadcasting would follow the same pattern. Whatever openings were provided in secular broadcasting, Rome would preserve its own, wholly-owned channels. Much of Southern Europe remained a Catholic fortress. In Spain and Portugal, Church and State dealt with each other on privileged terms. In Italy, however, there had been bitter confrontations over the secular power of the papacy. As things turned out, the independent status of Vatican City neatly fitted the radio era. In 1910, Marconi built a transmitter for the Pope. Alongside the concordats, accomodations and silences of the turbulent twentieth century, the Jesuit-managed Vatican Radio has given the Church an international voice that neither Fascism nor Communism has been able to drown.

In Catholic Europe, the Church has been primarily involved in its own mass media. The Polish Church was victim of forty years of radio silence but its print media helped to herald a national resurrection. In Spain, public and private radio co-existed from the beginning. The allocation of frequencies means that private radio tends to be local but it nevertheless has five times more listeners. In the 1950s, some two hundred parish radio stations went on air. Today the COPE channel is a radio company with 110 broadcasting centres throughout Spanish territory. COPE is an institution of the Spanish Catholic Church. In Italy 500 of the 3,500 local radio stations have a religious orientation. Of the four to five hundred TV stations, forty-five are linked to the Catholic Church. The Paulist order was founded by Giacomo Alberione. It received papal approval in 1930. The *raison d'être* of the five-hundred-strong order remains to provide the Church with its own string of magazines, newspapers and broadcasting stations. With a weekly circulation of 1.2 million copies, the Paulists' *Famiglia Christiana* is the biggest religious magazine in Italy – and Europe. As well as running two local radios, the order manages *Telenova*, a regional television station in Milan. In October 1989 Timoteo Giaccardo, a Paulist, was beatified by Pope John Paul II.

It is almost always impossible to speak of a worldwide Roman Catholic attitude to broadcasting. From Vatican City has come a world service with the voice of the Pope. In North America, the highly-commercialised broadcasting system has left seventy-five million Catholics seriously under-represented in public broadcasting. On the other hand, in Central and South America, small

Church-owned local radio stations have been key factors in building the base communities that have, in turn, made possible a revival of the Catholic tradition. In the Philippines, the Church-owned *Radio Veritas* helped turn the tide against the Marcos government, while in Northern Europe, Roman Catholics play their part in ecumenical broadcasting structures.

With the Second Vatican Council, the Catholic Church as a whole adopted a much more affirmative attitude to the electronic media. The caution of *Vigilante Cura* was replaced by the Council document *Inter Mirifica*. The new electronic technology was declared to be "among the wonders" of God's world. No matter which country they represented, the Council fathers could not doubt that broadcasting had changed the world. It could be used by a Goebbels or it could be a powerful weapon for the Church. Vatican II inaugurated World Communication Day (the Sunday after Ascension Day). The recommendation for a new Commission for Social Communication was Vatican II's first action for improving the central administration in Rome. The choice of the Franciscan, Father Agnellus Andrew, as first President of the commission was decisive. He had been a senior BBC staff member and a pioneer of the public-service and increasingly ecumenical approach in British religious broadcasting. The commission's document *Communio e progressio* was largely the work of Agnellus Andrew, who had been made a bishop. A new value was placed on Christians working in public broadcasting.

Throughout the first seventy years of European public-service broadcasting, room was found for Christian apologists. For example, in Britain, C.S.Lewis made a major contribution. On the other hand, Evangelical Christians were largely excluded. Of course the line between evangelism and apologetics may be a fine one. Radio especially lends itself to argument, whimsy and parable. But it is far less happy (and so are its managers) with direct appeals for repentance and the implied suggestion that the Christianity of some listeners is deficient. In much of the continent, Catholicism has been culturally ·dominant but Lutherans, Calvinists and Anglicans have been equally unwelcoming to Evangelicals. Until relatively recently, their influence, even in the Protestant countries, has been small. Public broadcasting in Northern Europe favoured a broad, undogmatic but not necessarily unintelligent Christianity that would appeal to the widest possible audience. Public-service radio breathes on the air of pluralism. Therefore it finds it difficult to accommodate groups who have critical things to say about the national religious consensus. These religious groups, and they are not to be confused with religious minorities, have been consciously excluded, usually on the grounds that they do not represent a significant enough part of the national culture.

Evangelicals have failed the broadcasting fitness test because their operating style is deemed to be unsuited to a medium which, by its nature, is inclusive and non-sectarian. But, at the same time, two processes have been underway. Outside Europe, there has been a massive, almost worldwide investment in missionary radio. European Evangelicals, once small in number, have had an enormous influence outside Europe. Denied a broadcasting outlet in their own countries, they have looked outwards to the mission fields. Sweden's Nibra Radio, founded by the Pentecostalist minister Lewi Petrhus, started broadcasting from the Tangier free zone in 1955. It now has eighty production centres worldwide and, by buying airtime on eight short-wave and seventy-five FM stations, broadcasts to one hundred countries.

The state broadcasting monopolies have created a situation in which many 'home-grown' prophets feel unrecognised in their own country. Through missionary broadcasting, several evangelists have constituencies in far off places. They are experienced communicators and well-placed to exploit new broadcasting freedoms and opportunities. Secondly, the word 'Evangelical' is now used in so many ways that much of its meaning is obscured. Although it is still applied to any fundamentalist Protestant offering a 'hot gospel', it also denotes theologically restrained Anglicans and is even sometimes used of Roman Catholic enthusiasts. The Lausanne movement has led to a widening of the term. Many of today's Evangelicals are somewhat less wary of the ecumenical movement. Some are found in large groupings within the traditional denominations. On the other hand many belong to small fellowships. Some of them feel distinctly warmer towards Roman Catholics than they do towards liberal fellow-Protestants.

In most European countries the original local radio initiatives were quickly subsumed into government-created monopolies. The situation in the United States has been quite different. A free market, a tradition of minimum government regulation and a long history of Christian revivalism led to the early and inevitable birth of gospel radio. In any case, North America was simply too big for coast-to-coast broadcasting services. The national commercial networks did not make their appearance until the 1930s. These networks gave an inexpensive and preferential position to the mainline Protestant denominations, the Roman Catholic Church and the Jews. However, the gospel stations continued to be part of the media market place.

When North American religious broadcasting was deregulated, the effect on Evangelical fortunes was immense. Federal regulations still required religious airtime but henceforth it need not be *free* time. Inevitably, religious broadcasting passed into the hands of the highest bidder. The self-supporting frontier preacher could now become a Televangelist. Now he could pass round his ten-gallon hat – by television. Unfortunately, for the mainline Churches, this revolution in financing more or less coincided with important developments in satellite-to-cable television. The protectors of the Churches, the big three American networks, now faced serious competition.

Of course, the surge in Evangelical fortunes did not owe everything to broadcast deregulation. Since the Second World War, Evangelicals have gained strength in every part of the world. In Europe, the traditional Churches have seen a decline. North American commerce, language and mass entertainment has invaded every continent and, at the very least, this has certainly not made it more difficult for American preachers to be heard. European Evangelicals have seen unprecedented growth and are not unaware of their mighty transatlantic ally. Some have been praying for the broadcasting chains to be unlocked. Now they are poised to take advantage of new media freedoms as various forms of state control, in Eastern and Western Europe, are lifted.

Evangelicals and Roman Catholics alike share the conviction that radio and television are gifts of God and the latest tools for building the kingdom. Some Evangelicals would go further. Broadcasting might be the final means of preaching the gospel to every creature. "We live in the final seconds of endtime" says evangelist Morris Cerullo ('an anointed and faithful servant of God' who 'for nearly thirty years... has cared for the spiritual needs of Great Britain.') "What we do to reach the lost souls of this world, we must do now! Our God-given object is to reach the world, and the modern miracle of advanced satellite technology enables Morris Cerullo World Evangelism to reach *more* people at an accelerated pace through the global satellite network".

However, in contrast to those who affirm the new electronics, there are also Christians who cannot escape the conviction that the mass media represses and regiments people. It is a fear and an idea that has currency worldwide and not just with paid-up Neo-Marxist semioticians. But the idea only thrives in patches. The result is often a lack of communication between communication experts. The World Association for Christian Communication (WACC) provides a case in point. For some years the WACC view of the mass media has been cautious to say the least. The Association has become a focus for many Christians worldwide who have seen at first hand how indigenous cultures can be swamped by foreign media. "The war against Nicaragua has been a war against social change, and alternative communications have played an important role in the struggle for peace with justice." WACC is a rallying point for people who protest at the one-way flow of news and values *out* of the industrialised countries and *into* the rest of the world. WACC's finest hour was the publication (with UNESCO) of the Sean MacBride report urging a New World Information and Communication Order.

Perhaps, the problem for WACC is a communication problem. The London-based organisation is a worldwide beacon to those who can see the light of liberation. However, some of its basic assumptions leave other Christians, including English prelates and Scottish divines, in an advanced state of bewilderment. The reaction of British clergymen may not be too important. But, if it really is true, as the Argentinian educator José Miguez-Bonino declared to WACC's 1989 congress in Manila, that "the system of oppression worldwide seeks to silence the poor by creating an atmosphere of terror and expropriating and monopolising the means of communication", then perhaps it should be made clear that he is not talking about the BBC World Service.

So what does religious broadcasting do? Is it part of a system of capitalist oppression? Does it simply demonstrate life in an old ecclesiastical dog? So what are the various levels at which broadcasting works? What do Churches achieve by being part of the broadcasting crew? What would happen if they jumped ship? In Western Europe less than half a century ago, television viewers were few in number. In their pre-televisual innocence, children saw things in black and white. My third picture is another childhood memory and comes from the days when comic papers still thrived. One of the British comics, the *Eagle* was built on the weekly adventures of Dan Dare and his assistant Digby and their evil adversary the Mekon, the ruler of the bad half of the planet Venus. The Mekon was a nasty little green fellow with a huge head. His legs were tiny, presumably because his sedentary ancestors had watched too much television and had stopped walking. The silver-haired Digby was a Yorkshireman. There was a special Venusian telephone system. It could transmit the whole person and not just the voice. Each molecule made its separate journey to the receiving phone box. When Digby transmitted himself to the other side of the planet, he would arrive in one piece, miraculously reassembled. But sometimes there would be a technical hitch. To his considerable annoyance he would arrive upside down and he would have to be rescued by Dan Dare. Something of the same notion can be found in TV's *Star Trek* with "Beam me up, Scotty".

Is electronic religion the same thing as real religion? Mercifully, religious broadcasters are still some way from physically popping out of the box! But that is what some of them would like to do. "If I could visit you personally, I would do so," cries America's Oral Roberts. In the meantime, he asks each interested viewer to make do with "this handkerchief which my right hand has touched". Europeans too have been known to try to replicate real flesh and blood events. In a famous and unrepeated experiment, Nordic broadcasters presented an international media version of the eucharist. A programme, recorded in Iceland, invited viewers in five countries and at different hours, to break their own bread and participate in an ethereal sacrament. Many years earlier, there had been enormous misgivings about the first Finnish radio service. ("Will drunks be disrespectful when they hear the prayers?") When the service was eventually transmitted from Tampere, it was received with the utmost seriousness. Groups of Finns, prayerful and participatory, gathered round their wireless sets and joined in the singing.

From the beginning, religious broadcasting was understood as the transmission of something real and potent. In Ireland, when the mass was first broadcast, it was only on the fictional understanding that this would be a service to the housebound and the infirm. In no way would it discharge the faithful from their churchgoing obligations. In country after country, there were heated arguments about the rights and wrongs of specially contrived studio services. Sometimes, there was resistance to the idea of airing any prayers at all, in case the wrong kind of people tuned in. ("Why cast pearls before swine?") Broadcasting did not do anything different. It extended the circle. Like a father, the King could talk to his Empire. President Roosevelt could invite every Tom, Dick and Harry to his White House fireside. The Protestant preacher believed that at last he had found a way to communicate with Calvin's invisible Church.

References

[1] *Les Rites et la Télévision.* See Bibliography.

[2] Some of Thorleif Pettersson's arguments can be found in English in the *Journal for the Scientific Study of Religion.* 1986, vol. 25: 391–409.

CHAPTER 4

Television without frontiers

The next picture was shared by all of us. One unusually visible Calvinist had brought things to a head. He was the pastor of Timosoara in Transylvania. It was Christmas and the 1980s had only hours to run. The holiday television schedules had been fixed long ago. Between the Christmas movies, we caught tantalising glimpses of a revolution by television. The pictures were picked up by Rumania's neighbours and then sent on to us by satellite. For once, a camera had told nothing but the truth. Ceausescu's angry face revealed that he could be cornered. No amount of audio dubbing could hide the fury of the crowd. The fighting citizens of Bucharest had one objective, the TV station. Unlike some uprisings, there was no Bastille, no Winter Palace. The TV station became the seat of government. Then came the video *fait accompli*. It was shown over and over again. It was not meant for us but for a Rumanian version of Doubting Thomas. "Only if I see the bullet holes in his chest will I believe." Television made belief possible. The tyrant had been put to death; proof, in pictures, that a nightmare could end.

"Please, Ivan, go home" says the polite Lithuanian placard to the Russians – but why say it in English? Television's new power to cross frontiers is now taken for granted. Using satellites like mirrors, reporters can bounce their pictures back to base in a fraction of a second. At the same time, tens of millions of European viewers can now choose from a variety of foreign television stations. A cable subscriber in Lausanne can switch to the British BBC as easily as she can the Italian RAI. Her uncabled sister in

Geneva is unimpressed. For many years she has been able to pick up three French TV channels. Not too far away in her village, Aunt Marie has no television choices. She too is uncabled and the mountains prevent her from receiving anything but *Télévision Suisse Romande*.

Medium-wave radio and 'terrestrial' television does not always travel well. Nevertheless it has not been possible, in Europe's mosaic of countries, to shape each broadcasting service so that it neatly fits the frontiers of politics and language. The British are an exception. Europeans in their tens of millions live near frontiers and they have ready access to foreign broadcasting. In the borderlands, very significant numbers have been able to see for themselves that the grass can be greener on the other side. For years East Germans turned to Western stations. Estonians have looked north to their cousins in Helsinki. Every evening the increasingly less compliant Albanians turn their home-made aerials to Italy, Greece or Yugoslavia. Some overspills (from Moscow, Hilversum, Monte Carlo and the Vatican) have been quite deliberate. Radio Luxembourg and the North Sea radio pirates were commercial attempts to cross frontiers. And, of course, in its time, the continent has had to endure a massive amount of propaganda and misinformation. Broadcasting within Europe has not always been nation speaking peace unto nation.

But there has been no *European* broadcasting, except perhaps during the Second World War, when most of the continent tuned to London. For most of the broadcasting era, while borderline viewers and short-wave amateurs and medium-wave linguists have had direct reception from abroad, most people have preferred to tune to their own country's radio and television. Despite the relative ease of receiving alternatives, most of the people for most of the time have chosen to rely on their own national broadcasting gatekeeper. Of course a primary reason has to be linguistic, but language is not the whole answer. Along the Belgian/French and the Belgian/Dutch borders, there are no language barriers but most Belgian viewers still tune in to Brussels. Dublin has some of the most talented radio presenters in Europe but RTE has relatively few listeners north of the border. Whatever else they disagree about, Northern Irish Catholics and Protestants seem to share the same tastes in radio and television. The general rule seems to be that consumers will stay loyal to their own national broadcasting unless their age group or interest group is ignored and unless a cross-border station offers a better technical standard, as does the BBC to Donegal.

But broadcasting across frontiers has an increasingly important place on the European agenda. Part of the reason can be found in the simple trigonometry of satellite broadcasting. Television signals find it difficult to bend! But an artificial earth satellite in fixed ('geo-stationary') orbit, 33,000 kilometres above the equator, provides a 'bouncing board' – a mirror that can reflect signals back on to a huge area. It is as if a tightly-focused flashlight is pointed at a football. The result is an ellipse (a 'footprint') of light. So two species of broadcasting now co-exist in Europe. The original, terrestrial broadcasting still has to take account of every range of hills. At the same time, the new satellite technology works from a more advantageous angle. Huge areas – Central Europe or Scandinavia or any other regional group of countries – can now be illuminated from one source in the sky. The USSR's *Statsionor 12* satellite has a stupendous footprint that covers half the world; Africa, Europe and most of Asia. Nowadays it carries Ted Turner's CNN which, as far as world news is concerned, is already a one-world channel. The Atlanta-based CNN is watched by the parliamentarians, dictators and opinion-formers of ninety-one countries. Journalists covering the events in Tienanmen Square were able to return to their hotel rooms and see the action. CNN is doing by television what the BBC once did by radio. Against heavy odds, Turner began to 'globalize' in 1980.

The beam from a satellite can be received in one of two ways. Signals go either to a single antenna serving any number of individual subscribers or, cutting out the 'middle man' – the cable operator, the signals go direct to the viewer's own receiving equipment (DBS). Cable and DBS are competitors in many parts of Europe. In North America the situation is different. Cable has a much longer history. It began in the mountains of Colorado as a supplement to terrestrial television; a way of guaranteeing reception in difficult areas. In Montreal, perhaps the most comprehensively cabled city in the world, cable was first introduced as a means of receiving television from the United States. Nowadays American cable broadcasting has to be understood as 'satellite-to-cable'. Real DBS has only become possible with the new generation of higher-powered satellites because these, in turn, make small domestic receiving dishes a possibility.

The extent of cabling in European countries varies greatly. In Belgium cable reaches 98 per cent of the population. In the Netherlands, the figure is only slightly lower. Sweden is fast approaching a situation where one third of the country is cabled. After a very slow start, the British cable companies have had a fresh injection of North American capital. On 1st July, 1990 some 600,000 British homes were passed by broadband cable. At the same time, Britain's Cable Authority was processing franchise applications that would result in broadband capacity being made available, at least 'in the road', to 14.5 million homes. Most countries have many years to go before their cable industry reaches capacity. Despite its considerable investment in interactive telephone services, Frenchmen have shown little interest in acquiring cable.

Because a cable system is fed by a number of different satellites, cable at present offers a greater variety of programmes than DBS. A fibre-optic cable system could offer each customer a choice of forty or fifty channels as well as interactive banking and community services. Some see DBS as a stop-gap. But it is too early to say if the rivalry will end with an outright winner. Both reception systems will co-exist in Europe well into the next century. The cost of cabling every single village and country lane may always remain uneconomic. Perhaps it will end up as a supplementary service in situations where cabling is expensive or difficult. It will soon be possible for domestic DBS dishes to be smaller. Less obtrusive, transparent models have already been announced. Before too long they may not need to be fixed to the outside of a building.

But other, shorter-term questions remain about the future of European DBS. The continent has three quite different satellite transmission technologies which will continue to be used until one, or even two, of them collapse under the weight of market or political pressure. Rupert Murdoch's Sky Television makes use of one of the two Astra intermediate satellites and broadcasts in the PAL 625 system. Owned by a Luxembourg-based company, Astra has not been officially designated as a DBS satellite. Nor is it high-powered. But in an industry where positioning is all-important, Astra was available. It was up and running. Somewhat bulky receiving dishes have enabled Sky to be first in the race for DBS.

It was confidently (and wrongly) expected that PAL would be gradually phased out. The future in Europe seemed to belong to the state-of-the-art D-MAC system. Japanese technology would be kept at bay. By the end of the century, much of the continent should be moving over to high-definition (1250–line) TV. Screens will be re-proportioned in a new '9 x 4' shape. Interestingly, the British mini-series *The Ginger Tree* was shot in high-definition TV but, whatever the politicians decree, an inter-European movement towards HDTV is likely to be delayed until the major manufacturers can agree common standards. The latest D-MAC transmission system could easily handle the changeover to HDTV, with room to spare for digital sound, eight high-quality audio channels and a data package. Alone in Europe, Britain's British Satellite Broadcasting (BSB) is the only satellite operator to use D-MAC. Yet another system is used by a number of European satellite broadcasters. Known as D/2 MAC, it has a somewhat reduced bandwidth. But some operations, including the Copernicus satellite, are breaking ranks and giving a new lease of prolonged active life to PAL.

In European satellite broadcasting 1992 is likely to mean nothing. Confusion will continue to reign. The officially approved DBS satellites have an internationally agreed position above the equator. Britain's (and therefore BSB's) position is 31 degrees West. The Astras are in a different constellation of satellites. So as well as using a different technology, the Sky signal comes from a different direction and consumers face the well-advertised problem of needing two separate dishes. However, before too long, there may be a fixed-aerial on the market that can receive from widely separated satellites. Separate receiving circuitry would still be required. In Germany, DM 734 will buy a dish and convertor capable of receiving ninety-nine programmes.

Satellites were foreseen by Arthur C. Clarke, a European and a dreamer with a knack of seeing things clearly. The launching capacity which enables satellites to be put into position is a direct result of the research into the wartime V2 rocket. Much of the huge satellite insurance risk is carried in London. But life is not simple for those who want a new and peaceful Europe united by satellite broadcasting. The technological mismatching is an unnecessary complication, especially for DBS. It is an outward and visible sign that European electronic manufacturing capacity is divided and fragmented. But technological differences can always be overcome. Europe's cultural diversity and the nature of broadcasting itself are likely to remain the fundamental issues.

In a *'Europe des patries'*, how can broadcasting give a worthwhile and simultaneous service to different national cultures and language groups? How can the individual cultures of the European states and regions be protected from the Anglo-Americans? Could there be a non-commercial European channel? In some Brussels' corridors, the thought still lingers that the European Community could or should sponsor a degree of trans-border broadcasting. It would not rely solely on advertising support and would be driven by a public-service philosophy. Jean Dondelinger, the French Commissioner with responsibility for the audio-visual industries, is behind the idea, as was his Italian predecessor, Carlo Ripadimeana. Perhaps it is a pipedream. It would be politically impossible for a Euro-Channel to be anything but 'unscrambled' DBS which could also be accessed by cable station. Such a channel would have to hitch-hike on the back of an existing commercial network.

Some forms of television work well across frontiers. Western rock music is already international and nurtures parallel cultures in most countries of the world. Sport too knows few frontiers and is essentially visual – or at least the audio commentary that reinforces sport comes from an unseen source. But the current satellite channels that aspire to be European are being held back, not simply by language, but by the enormous difficulty of devising advertising with a European appeal. Coca-Cola is an exception to a general rule that advertisements are most effective when they are created for one particular country. Very few internationally-marketed products could succeed behind one single, multinational advertising campaign. This makes it very difficult for an advertising-supported European channel to be sustained.

One commercial European satellite network (using Eutelsat) has already been and gone. It is said of the ill-fated Europa channel that it came too early, before the continent was ready for it. Given another five years, it might have succeeded. The real reason for the failure of Europa was that it was the child of a marriage of several national commercial networks (British, Dutch, German, Portuguese and Italian). In order to survive it would have needed to compete aggressively against its own parents. Instead, it faced advertising bans and difficulties, particularly in the Dutch market. Unlike many of the later satellite services, Europa TV was based on a number of public-service broadcasting principles.

The millionaire, Piet Derksen, had the rights to two hours of religious broadcasting each Sunday on Europa TV. So what of those who dream dreams of presenting the Christian gospel from the sky? One evangelist from a studio somewhere in Europe could look half a continent in the eye. Or rather, and the distinction is very important, half the continent could look in the evangelist's eye. If these are the endtimes – and the time is short – what better way to fulfil the great commission to preach the gospel to every creature? Indeed, an imaginative look at the 'winged creatures' of the Book of Revelation might even suggest that there is more to a satellite than meets the eye. Could not Europe's mighty Catholic tradition, with a religious culture and common allegiance that unites tens of millions in every land, be re-focused by satellite broadcasting? How could a Lithuanian Catholic fail to be encouraged by a direct, televisual link with Lourdes, with Fatima and with Rome? Thanks to satellites, it is now possible for the Pope himself personally to lead the prayers of the faithful – from the Atlantic to the Urals.

But, with or without the Apocalypse, satellites are not all they seem. They have not simplified television. They have not created a visual version of short-wave radio. Signal reception is a complicated business. Satellite television itself has become hugely expensive. BSB has committed four hundred million pounds. Rupert Murdoch seems to be drawing his bottom line under five hundred million. So access to television is ever more costly. Within both DBS and cable television, there will be an increasing trend for the most palatable items on the menu to be reserved for those who are prepared to pay-as-they-view. Nevertheless, satellites seemed to be the answer to a missionary's prayer. First of all, satellites had the capacity to break the stranglehold of the national monopolies and to offer the preacher a new freedom, *sans frontières*, and to behave as if there is neither Jew nor Greek. The truth is that media power has indeed been redistributed – but not in the direction of those who simply want to talk to the continent on television.

The satellites themselves are largely financed by an invisible subsidy – a growing, commercial data traffic comfortably conceealed within their massively high frequencies. Then again, although the national broadcasting corporations have been bruised, they have certainly not collapsed. Some are partners in satellite broadcasting or engage in joint ventures with the new entrepreneurs. The national systems are destined to contract and some of their jewels, especially their sporting jewels, have been pawned or stolen. For perfectly good advertising reasons, most of the new satellite operations are not idealistically European. Indeed, BSB is so determinedly British that it uses a broadcasting technology that is unavailable in other European countries. With a spectacularly successful financial record, the Swedish TV3 satellite channel (via Astra) is one of the strongest pressures on the Swedish government to reach a quick decision on allowing advertising within its own nationally-regulated broadcasting. So far from facing a new generation of television moguls to whom national frontiers mean nothing, the older corporations now face a new and less-restricted breed of national competition.

Up to now most of Europe's new satellite channels have shown little interest in religious broadcasting. All but the maverick satellite companies are, at least loosely, accountable to national institutions but they stand or fall on the single and harsh judgment of the marketplace. Sometimes, their exclusive coverage of high-profile sporting events is of the highest quality; a loss-leader to persuade waverers that a dish would be a good investment. On the other hand, some European channels rely heavily on dated American movies. Satellite broadcasting offers a product. There is very little incentive to provide a diverse range of programmes. Survival depends entirely on audience ratings and advertising revenue. Not unreasonably, what the customer wants from cable or dish is television that cannot be found anywhere else. The fact that many national broadcasting corporations have some continuing obligation to provide religious programmes means that the new satellite alternative has an extra excuse for leaving religion well alone.

National churches have next to no input into the world of satellite broadcasting. But there are success stories. Nils-Gøren Wetterberg, the communication director of the Swedish Lutheran Church, made a request for some religious programming to the senior management of the TV3 channel. He was rebuffed. So he made a direct approach to New York – to Ian Steinmann, owner of the London-based company. The result was an agreement for a series of fifty-two Sunday morning meditations in music and poetry. Some observers claim to see a new trend towards quality in satellite broadcasting. The new Scandinavian TV4 channel has set itself some widely-publicised public-service obligations. At the early planning stage, there were requests to representatives of several national churches for religious programming ideas. From September 1990, a one-hour Sunday programme is planned on religious and existential issues.

But on the whole the early years have not seen much recognition of the European Churches. Each Sunday Sky Television gives two showings of the *Hour of Power*, Dr. Robert Schuller's weekly celebration of the power of positive thinking from his Los Angeles Crystal Cathedral. Well-made programmes from the religious fringes have had a surprisingly good airing. Superchannel, a company with European pretensions, provided time for the Worldwide 'Church' of God. For the nineties, Sky News has added a monthly discussion programme *Challenge*, hosted by Clifford Longley, religious correspondent of another of Mr. Murdoch's media *The Times*.

Europe's satellite capacity is growing fast. At the beginning of 1990, thirty-two broadcast channels were available from satellites. Within twelve months, this figure more than doubled to seventy-seven. By 1996, there could well be 160 separate satellite channels. This bountiful over-provision stands in sharp contrast to an acute and growing shortage of European-made television programmes. The new Europe may well be a huge market, the biggest in the world, but its television programme production industry is underdeveloped. The problem is new but acute. American and Japanese penetration of the market is large enough to stunt the growth of European audio-visual production. Sixty per cent of all film distribution within Europe is American-controlled. Of the 11,000 hours of children's cartoons screened in Europe each year, only 350 hours are 'home produced'.

The single media market will continue to be fragmented. Western Europe is, in fact, largely made up of five separate media markets (Germany, Britain, France, Italy and Spain). Each is capable of a certain financial self-sufficiency. But countries, large or small, show little interest in working against the backdrop of a single European media landscape. Although Europeans manage to export cars, cheese and whisky to each other, a market-resistance to foreign television programmes is simply taken for granted. For example, of all the programmes made in the United Kingdom in a year, only six per cent are ever viewed in any other country.

There is now a chronic under-production of homegrown programmes and the growing mis-match between supply and demand may never be solved in Europe's favour. There is a disharmony over programme rights which makes it very difficult for independent producers to build up their bank balances. Media education in Europe lags far behind what is readily available in the United States. Nowhere in Europe can a media executive take a higher degree in the crucial areas of distribution and marketing. The problem is beginning to be recognised. At least one British university (the University of Kent) is making plans for an MBA degree in Media Management. Language is obviously the biggest single factor in limiting the free flow of programmes, and European countries vary greatly in their acceptance of dubbing and subtitling. But if producers are to take advantage of 1992, many more programmes will have to be made for more than one language group. Italians are a great exception but very many European producers are lethargic when it comes to tackling the issue of language conversion. Meanwhile, on the other side of the Atlantic, perfectionist distributors even dub from English into American!

For a continent that is supposed to be growing together, there is remarkably little interest in television from across the internal frontiers. Even the much derided 'Euro-puddings' are in short supply. On the other hand, Californian pudding can be sold in every European country while high-quality programmes like *Otto*, the popular German series, rarely find an outside buyer. This is not nationalism. It is more a matter of national taste. But the situation is made worse by the structural weakness and fragmentation in the European audio-visual industry and by the fact that European television is still heavily subsidised by the North American viewer. While most American television is made for a world market, seventy per cent of all production costs are found within the United States. Consequently American programmes in Europe are numerous and cheap as well as popular. Edith Cresson, France's European Affairs minister is strongly in favour of protectionism. "What would remain of our cultural identity if audio-visual Europe consisted of European consumers sitting in front of Japanese TV sets showing American programmes?" When it comes to religious programming, some Christian voices are less certain. "The Devil has played an anti-American card", said Gareth Littler of the Campaign for Christian Standards in Society. Professor Cees Hamelink of the University of Amsterdam and a wise man of WACC has another view. "The real threat to culture isn't Americanisation", he argued in *Newsweek*. "It's commercialisation."

Media protectionism will be difficult to enforce. A audio-visual 'Fortress Europe' may simply mean that Hollywood (like Disneyland) will move, lock, stock and barrel, into the Old World. And in any case some countries are more defensive than others. Compared with the rest of western Europe, a common language has not made Britain especially reliant on American material. Britain has been *relatively* resistant to US penetration because it has a strong national television culture and, up to now, an effective system of regulation which limits imports. By the same token, Britain is highly resistant to non-English language imports. On the other hand, the number of co-productions between France, Germany and Italy is increasing. In 1988, Europe bought $700 million worth of programmes from the USA. The European Co-production Association is one example of a co-ordinated attempt at redressing the transatlantic balance. ECA is a consortium made up of seven European public service television companies. It was set up to produce television fiction for a Europe-wide audience and with a special emphasis on long-running series. By 1990, fifty-two programme hours per year were being produced with an output that included *Eurocops, The Strauss Dynasty* and *The Black Virgin.*

"Why can't I export this series?" complained a Danish producer at a meeting in London arranged by the European Television Forum. "Is the scenery too Danish? Do we Danes have two heads?"

"Put Dustin Hoffman in the leading role and you can be as Danish as you like," came the cynical but realistic German reply.

Seventy years ago, on both sides of the Atlantic, the beginnings of broadcasting were similar. And these beginnings were truly local because they were often commercial. Wireless sets do not grow on trees. Pittsburg, Pennsylvania, had a station (KDKA) because it also had a manufacturer (Westinghouse). Similarly in England, Station 2MT grew up in the shadow of Marconi's Chelmsford company. But American and European broadcasting soon took different roads. North America followed the path of regulated free enterprise. And American geography and ideology combined to ensure that local broadcasting remained the norm. But European broadcasting, whether in the democracies or the one-party states, has been organised on a national pattern. It has been made to serve as a major expression of national identity – a role from which printing and publishing have often been able to escape.

But although radio and television have often emphasised frontiers, they have not been able to subdivide and nationalise religion and culture. There have been opposite and stronger currents and they have been flowing from across the Atlantic. Since the war, American mass entertainment has been carried round the world by the electronic media and has been one of the most important building blocks for history's first global culture. Even the stronger and undivided Europeans, free from such horrors as Ceasescu and the Berlin Wall, cannot pretend that their new European home is an island. There can be no exclusively European media policies. The new unity is not being drawn on a blank piece of paper but in a world of long-standing international relationships and, let it be said, in a century in which Americans have twice fought and died in the Old World. European identity is much talked about but more often in the context of a search rather than a self-evident reality. The question remains in many minds. Does this new Europe even exist except as an alliance of democracies and as a marketplace?

As far as broadcasting legislation is concerned, the European Community is motivated by a mixture of openness and protectionism. In 1989 the Community adopted a 'Television without frontiers' Directive in order to create a Europe-wide broadcasting market. It contained a recommendation for fifty-one per cent European content. From the autumn of 1991, the Directive becomes a political, but legally unenforceable, commitment for the member states. Audio-visual Eureka is the rather unlikely title for a co-operation framework between the EEC Commission and a wider group of twenty-six European countries. Unlike the EEC Directive, the Convention on Transfrontier Television of the 25–nation Council of Europe is very much an exercise in consumer protection, defining minimum standards. There are no references to children's or religious programmes. The Convention's only excursion into altruism is when it covers the same ground as the EEC Directive and recommends that half of Europe's airtime should be filled by locally-made programmes.

As a first step, the EEC Commission sponsored a pilot Audio-visual Initiative to support work in dubbing, animation and script-writing. In 1990, at the end of the pilot stage, the EEC Commission presented the Council of Ministers with a five-year proposal for spending 250,000,000 ecus to stimulate production and distribution partnerships. The EEC media action programme is impressive, if only for its acronymic inventiveness. There is MEDIA (Measures to Encourage the Development of the Audio-visual Industry) which will continue to create trans-frontier production networks. Then there is EFDO (the European Film Distribution Office) and EVE (*Espace Video European*). The pilot project BABEL is particularly well-named. BABEL stands for Broadcasting Across the Barriers of European Languages. Then comes EURO-AIM (for the independent sector), SCRIPT (for scenarios and pre-production work), CARTOON (for animation) and MAP-TV (to exploit Europe's rich heritage of archive material). The excruciatingly-named 'MAC/Packet Directive' (technical standards) will require updating in 1991.

The European audio-visual industry is changing fast. Over the next ten years, the EEC's audio-visual turnover will increase by ten billion ecus to thirty-five billion. Western Europe, at least, has a firm timetable for lowering its internal barriers. However, the penetration of foreign material is likely to continue. Then there is a new and unexpected East European dimension. Long before *perestroika*, Poles, Czechs and Hungarians had some of the world's best film-makers. Everything seems to be changing and at the same time, broadcasting technology has made it possible to bracket half a continent. Meanwhile, the West European countries have seen a decade of broadcasting devolution – more and more channels licensed for ever-smaller local units.

Amid much change and confusion, new questions are being asked about one of the oldest sub-departments of European broadcasting. In the East, the Churches are seizing long-lost opportunities. Within six months of the fall of the Ceasescus, the Rumanian Orthodox Church had put in an application for its own radio station. But in the West, religious producers are having to work harder for their place on the airwaves. Meanwhile, as more and more satellite and local channels become available, some Christians are hoping for a piece of the action. What place will there be for religion in the culture of the new Europe? Is trans-frontier religious broadcasting a desirable possibility? Or should the sower confine his seed to his own separate plot in the European jigsaw? Like Captain Queeg, there will always be Christians who prefer to talk to their world through some well-positioned Tannoy.

However, for most churchpeople, the important dimension is not continental nor even national. It is the chapel at the end of the road, or the house group over the hill. Only by belonging to a congregation does a wider membership of a universal, supranational Church make sense. For others, that great army of occasional visitors, the large-scale ecclesiastical institutions mean even less. The local church building is a place to turn to on family occasions. But only very rarely have broadcasters bothered with St. Gregory's-down-the-Road. Perhaps frontier-crossing should be left to the birds. Possibly, Christians should put their eggs into a small basket that is people-proportioned. Instead of following every technological or international red herring, why not put St. Gregory's on the map?

Technically, radio and television can work at many levels: international, continental, national, regional, local or community. But that does not mean that, for religious broadcasting, all levels are equally appropriate. But "the 21st century will be spiritual or it will not be", said Malraux. In this age of technological revolution and the building of a new European home, what will be the European faith? If the new Europe is to be something that is more than a market it will need, in Bergson's words, a *supplément d'âme*. Will this spiritual ingredient come from Brussels or from some religious commissioner in space? What are the options for Europe's religious broadcasting? Or rather, what are the choices that make theological sense?

CHAPTER 5

Christian investments across borders

In the geography of satellite broadcasting, London is well-placed. Archbishop John Foley, the Vatican's top media man, came to London's Dockland for the biggest satellite broadcast in history. It marked the opening of the Roman Catholic Marian Year.

From Rome, Pope John Paul II ushered in his fourteen months of special intercession to Mary with a multilingual recitation of the Rosary. Twenty-three broadcast satellites linked the Pope to an estimated 1.5 billion people and to shrines dedicated to the Virgin in five continents.

Master control was in the cavernous Limehouse Studios. Orchestrating one thousand technicians throughout the world was Tony Verna, the man who directed *Live Aid, Sport Aid* and the Los Angeles Olympics.

During the broadcast, the Archbishop sat in the darkened Limehouse control area before a wall of flickering TV sets. Paintings of the Madonna were beamed in from Paraguay, Senegal, India and many other countries. The wall of TV monitors made a 21st-century iconostasis – a warm and glowing patchwork screen. In one rectangle of light, the Pope fingered his beads. Another square slowly filled with the weather-beaten features of Mother Teresa saying her rosary in Poland.

In Rome scarlet cardinals glided majestically. President Aquino prayed from Manila. Children laughed for the camera in Austria and Argentina.

"Dissolve the Pope," ordered Verna. "Give me Fatima! Where's Fatima?" Bending his waist and chopping the air in a rhythm of downbeats, the maestro's commands seemed to transform him into a kind of Marian metronome. "Fatima!" "Lourdes!" "Mariazell!" "Knock!" "Caacupe!" "Quebec!" "Dakar!" "Zaragoza!" "Lu-jan!" "Czestochowa!" "Washington D.C.!" In strictly-timed sequence, the icons flashed into Limehouse and off round the globe like colour slides.

"Now I control the world," laughed Verna but did not mean it. "Cue the choir!" *"Regina Caeli!"* The Romans obeyed. In another part of the building, a team of commentators, led by Archbishop Foley, translated the Pope's sermon. The hour had almost gone. Children of the world brought flowers to Our Lady. John Paul II burned incense before an icon which, according to the English-language commentator, could be a reproduction of St. Luke's original.

So much for my fourth picture; another memory. And it is still a vivid memory in the offices of the Pontifical Council for Social Communications in Vatican City. In the Council's offices in the Palazzo San Carlo, a real picture from that great day in Docklands hangs on the waiting-room wall. The Commission's President, Archbishop John Foley, speaks fondly of the talented Tony Verna. Could there be an encore one day? Very unlikely. The worldwide telecast was a million-dollar disaster. The BIC Corporation had underwritten a proportion of the cost. The contribution of the Catholic Church had been clearly spelt out. Verna had hoped to recoup the rest from video sales. In other respects too this colourful hour was a disappointment. It was well-received by Asian stations and American networks but the response by European public broadcasting was cautious and bureaucratic. Ironically, although the programme was controlled and up-linked from Limehouse, it was not carried live by any British station.

Vatican programmes have more success when they are more traditional or have a specific interest to one particular country. In November 1989, the first religious television programme was broadcast in Czechoslovakia. It was sent live by the Vatican Television Centre but Czechoslovak Television relayed only a part of the ceremony. Public reaction was so great that, one week later, a recording, complete and unabridged, was re-broadcast. Christmas and Easter masses from St. Peter's (up-linked by RAI) are carried by satellite to many countries. The 1989 Christmas Midnight Mass celebrated by Pope John Paul II was transmitted to fifty-two countries including, for the first time, East Germany and Hungary. A one-hour special, including excerpts from the Pope's Christmas message in St. Peter's Square, was shown in prime time in the Soviet Union on Christmas night.

The Council for Social Communications, the first concrete result of Vatican II, has a wide portfolio of tasks. For example, it oversees the Vatican Film Library which was founded by Leo XIII. Titles include *The Song of Bernadette* and *Going My Way*. To mark the twentieth anniversary of *Communio e progressio* in 1991, Archbishop Foley's office is now working on suggestions for an updated version. The Archbishop authorises all radio and television work within Vatican City but the Church's worldwide broadcasting service, Vatican Radio, is directly accountable to the Secretary of State. Two hundred and fifty hours of programmes are broadcast each week in thirty-four languages. The total output amounts to about one third of that of the BBC's external services. Despite a fifteen-million dollar loss in 1988, the 420 staff would like to do more and there are some big gaps in their coverage, notably Indonesia and Korea. The gaps matter to Vatican Radio's Jesuit Director, Father Pasquale Borgomeo. "Everyone deserves their own programme. To the Catholic Church, there are no fore-igners." Even before the age of *perestroika*, a public-service broadcasting philosophy had been adopted. "We are not conclu-sive like *Osservatore Romano*", says Father Borgomeo, a Neapolitan. "We tend to comment and reflect on world events. Things like the release of Nelson Mandela and International Women's Day. We are much more independent from what is generally regarded as religious. We have to win listeners just like any other station. The laws of creation are holy. Radio has its own laws and it has to be used according to its nature. People will not necessarily listen to us just because we have the bells of St. Peter's. If we really believe the Spirit, we have only to prepare and not invade."

Every word that the Pope speaks in public in any part of the world is kept on tape. There is even an international Dial-the-Pope telephone service. It costs the caller between $1.60 and $2.12 per minute and the message is changed every twenty-four hours. A powerful short-wave transmitter in the heart of Rome would be electronically disastrous. Seventeen miles from Rome, at Santa

Maria de Galeria, the Pope has a small enclave of sovereign territory for Vatican Radio's rotating transmitter. The impressive array of aerials are configured in the shape of a cross. They are rotated daily, sending Vatican Radio's call sign (the opening bars of *"Christus Vincit"*) to most parts of the globe. Up to now the reliance on short-wave broadcasting has been almost total. "It is a good emergency medium" says Pasquale Borgomeo. "But in future we will have to think about getting our material on to FM stations." Satellite relay will play a part. At present Vatican Radio's tapes for the Catholic Telecommunications Network of America (CTNA) travel by diplomatic bag! But not everything is short-wave. Pius XI was the first Pope to provide the citizens of Rome with their own local radio station. It broadcasts today in FM. The station sound is a discreet easy-listening mixture of soft pop and classical music. There are very few words; just the occasional two-minute 'thought'.

*

Not every Roman Catholic in the world is in step with the Church's official broadcasting work. In the Third World, most particularly in South America, local radio has been one of the key factors in building base communities. Many of Latin America's thousands of local stations have set out be a means of liberation from social oppression; to give a voice to the voiceless and, in some cases, to give a voice to liberation theology. In North America and Europe, however, problems arise on the other wing of the Catholic Church. On both sides of the Atlantic, there are Roman Catholics who are distressed that, to name but one, Vatican Radio is not Catholic enough. In the United States, Mother Angelica, a nun with powerful support and a coast-to-coast television ministry based in Alabama, preaches a folksy brand of very traditional, no-nonsense Catholicism. Three years ago Mother Angelica faced serious financial problems but she has defied the prophets and survived. Unlike the American religious orders, who followed a more ecumenical line, the United States Conference of Bishops seemingly preferred Mother Angelica's professional services to those of the new Interfaith VISN Network. But now, to the evident irritation of some of Vatican Radio's staff, Mother Angelica has brought her work to Rome. On the other hand, her backers believe that it is high time to have a Catholic traditionalist on the European airwaves who keeps to the (Catholic) straight and narrow.

An ally of Mother Angelica in her Roman adventure is the Dutch multi-millionaire Piet Derksen, owner of the *Center Parcs* leisure empire and the force behind *Lumen 2,000*. Derksen's influence is discussed in Chapter 8. He is a Charismatic Catholic and his media ambitions have been viewed with considerable suspicion by many European bishops. He is mending his fences with *Unda*, the Brussels-based Catholic broadcasters' association. He has done good work for lepers in Colombia. According to Ed Arons of *Lumen 2,000* "Two thousand Catholics are lost every day to the fundamentalists in South America." Using the media, Piet Derksen wants "to build a dam against Protestant fundamentalists". He is for Catholic evangelism. This is different from some other varieties because it preaches love and not hate. He is not against ecumenism, but not at any price. "A world-spanning satellite net, that is certainly my dream."

But what of the centre? Are there Roman Catholics who are neither liberation theologians or charismatic propagandists but who simply want the Church to be part of Europe's new broadcasting opportunities? Richard Schoonhoven is the Director of KRO, the Dutch Catholic station and, with twenty television hours each week, the fourth biggest broadcasting organisation in the Netherlands. In 1986 in Dublin, he addressed the first meeting of European Bishops with responsibility for the media and communication. On that occasion, he was negative about any idea of a European Catholic satellite channel. Four years later, in Fatima, Portugal, the Dutch broadcasting executive was again invited to address the 'Media Bishops'. This time, the representation was wider. Bishops and advisers came from nearly every European country, East and West. Richard Schoonhoven began with the bald statement that he had changed his mind. Time had moved on and a European Christian satellite service might just be feasible and appropriate.

Such a Christian station would be enormously expensive. The annual cost of providing ten hours of television each day could be £100 million. Advertising would have to be 'detached'. In other words, advertisers would have no direct influence on programme content. There would still be objections that a Christian channel would become a ghetto and give other broadcasters an excuse for neglect. Compared with any religious broadcasting previously undertaken in Europe, this new idea would involve a massive enlargement of scale. It could not be an all-religious channel.

Specifically religious programmes would have to be placed carefully and should take up no more than fifteen per cent of the total output. The venture would have to be built on the continent's cultural and religious diversity and (an interesting distinction) responsibility for programmes should be in the hands of Christians and not those of the Churches. One of the final resolutions of the Fatima Conference was to ask for a feasibility study into Richard Schoonhoven's suggestion.

If there were any doubts at Fatima, the cardinals and bishops kept them to themselves. Most of the West Europeans could sense the seriousness of the Dutchman's challenge. To the Lithuanians, Hungarians and Slovenians, whose brightest hope was a training scholarship in journalism or a second-hand TV camera, it must have seemed pie in the Western sky. Probably, Schoonhoven knew what his audience did not know. In the United States, not too many months before the Fatima Conference, some of the communication officials of the mainline Churches were dreaming similar dreams. One year ago, the VISN Channel seemed pie in the sky but, with the backing of well-endowed churches and the crucially important support of America's biggest cable operator, the ecumenical network's outlook has been transformed.

An important part of the Schoonhoven proposal on a European Christian station was that "divided Christianity should not be the starting point" for such an undertaking. But up to now, the world has not seen much of ecumenical satellite broadcasting. The Ecumenical Satellite Commission, which had the support of WACC's predecessor and *Unda* (the Roman Catholic Broadcasters' Association), came to a end as long ago as 1973. ESC sprang from Sodapax, the ecumenical initiative for peace and justice and one of the only two firm links that has ever existed between the Vatican and the World Council of Churches. However, in the mid-Seventies, ecumenical relations cooled and the bright hopes for beaming a united Christian message from Honolulu to the Pacific region fizzled out. Nowadays, there is an EESC (European Ecumenical Satellite Committee) which is related to WACC, the Lutheran World Federation and the World Council of Churches. It does useful work in Christian communication but it is only ecumenical in a pan-Protestant sense and it is only slightly concerned with satellites.

Indeed, the Churches of the Reformation face their own set of special difficulties when considering pan-European broadcasting. In the case of French Roman Catholics, it is conceivable (but not absolutely certain) that they would be interested in a religious broadcast from Rome. But would Anglicans watch a German *Kirchentag* or a Waldensian wedding? Perhaps they ought to do so but television audiences are not built on moral imperatives. The political achievement of the Reformation was to build national churches for the new nation states. In the first flush of reform, European Protestantism meant a great deal. Doctrine and preaching flowed across frontiers. Kings and princes, merchants and beggars were converted. Luther and Calvin, Knox, Cranmer and Agricola are all among the founders of modern Europe.

Nowadays to be a Protestant still means a great deal but to be a specially European Protestant means next to nothing (unless, of course, one is a minority Protestant in Latin Europe). It is not that the established Protestants of the North have no identity. They often have a very strong identity and can still claim the status of folk Churches in much of Scandinavia and even in parts of Britain and Germany. But, conceived in an Erastian embrace and spending their formative years in the creation of national languages and literatures, the identity of these Churches is national or it is nothing. After two centuries of colonisation and missionary work, most Protestant denominations (both the established and minority Churches) have stronger links with their co-religionists in other continents than they do with their fellow Europeans. So 'inter-European' Protestant television is almost a contradiction – or rather, it would mean no more than 'world' Protestant television. The Catholics have an international and visual liturgy and, of course, they have the Pope, Lourdes and Oberammergau. One day, in Robert Schuman, they may have a Euro-saint. Indeed, they have a collection of television icons. But, for the iconoclastic children of the Reformation, television icons are in rather short supply. And "Amen to that," cry Calvinists, Baptists and some Anglicans. "What the world needs from Protestants is not icons but the word of God. The gospel that Luther discovered and Wesley rediscovered will more than suffice for the television age."

As far as the radio age is concerned, there has already been a great deal of Evangelical activity. The fact that broadcasting has been regulated and monopolised by European governments has not prevented European Christian broadcasters from filling the world's airwaves with programmes. Sweden's IBRA Radio is but one example. The station began broadcasting in 1955 from the Tangier free zone. The idea of the founder, the Pentecostal pastor Lewi Petrhus, was to reach Sweden. Nowadays IBRA has eighty production centres worldwide and buys airtime on seventy-five FM and eight short-wave stations. Facing a large world map that lights up every one of IBRA's radio outposts, the director, Fred Nyman, claims that up to a quarter of a million conversions are made each year. In one year alone, in Tanzania, up to ten new churches have been founded as a result of broadcasting work. IBRA has a budget of nineteen million crowns and most of it is provided by the Swedish Pentecostal congregations. Many of the missionary programme schedules could well be described as 'public service'. There are programmes for children, nursing mothers and farmers as well as direct preaching. Many Protestant Churches have been involved in missionary radio. Many support the Far East Broadcasting Association which transmits from the Seychelles. After the revolution in Ethiopia, the Lutherans' Radio Voice of the Gospel was evicted from Addis Ababa. In its heyday the station had a very considerable influence. Now this much-respected missionary institution has met a strange European fate. It now lives on in radio silence, subsumed into the communication department of the Lutheran World Federation whose office is close to the World Council of Churches in Geneva.

Missionary radio worldwide has at least the same capacity as the BBC External Services. Most of the European-funded stations have looked outwards to Africa, Asia and the Pacific. Some have tried to be heard in Europe and, after the construction of the Iron Curtain, several have for many years, beamed powerful signals to encourage the Christians of the East. Trans World Radio was founded in the United States. It also began transmitting to Europe from Tangier but then it moved to Monte Carlo. TWR is now forging its own, clearer, European identity. It has enjoyed mixed fortunes in Western Europe. In Britain it has had relatively few listeners. However, in West Germany (perhaps because Evangelicals, on the one hand, and the *Evangelisches Kirche*, on the other, are distinctly polarised) TWR is well-known and influential. It has been closely associated with the impressive media centre at Wetzlar, north of Frankfurt.

Dave Adams, European Director of TWR, is based in Hilversum. He has had his own African experience and is more sanguine about 'conversion statistics'. He fears that many of those who are flocking to the new African Churches may be doing so for superficial reasons. Closely involved in many inter-European media initiatives, Dave Adams says that TWR has "always tried to work openly with Eastern Europe". Now that the Curtain has been raised, TWR, like Vatican Radio, is hoping for time on local FM stations. In Hungary this has already begun to happen. The short-wave transmissions will continue but Dave Adams hopes that "within two years", fifty per cent of TWR's 'Eastern' material will be made within each receiving country. Perhaps the most spectacular openings have been in the USSR itself. TWR has opened its own studios in Moscow, Minsk and Kiev. The management is local and a mobile radio van has also been provided and three 'suitcase kits'. Some of the costs will be met by hiring out the new Soviet-based facilities.

West European Evangelicals are grouped in at least four loose structures. The European Evangelical Communicators Association (EURECA) serves established Christian broadcasters and Christians in the general media. Broadly associated with Eureca is the Christian European Visual Media Association (CEVMA) which tries to serve the interests of film and television producers. Alpha-Omega links the television work of the European Pentecostal Churches. European Religious Broadcasters (ERB) takes a particular interest in trans-frontier television and has links with the United States. Indeed, it takes as its model the powerful American grouping National Religious Broadcasters (NRB), the Televangelists' 'trade association'. Leaders of NRB are usually present at ERB's annual convention. Immediately after their 1990 convention, many ERB leaders moved on to Budapest to consider media-possibilities in Eastern Europe. Many of the Dutch, German, British and Norwegian members speak of their long exclusion from national broadcasting. Most of them are well-prepared for new freedoms. As well as being the pastor of a well-attended church in Altensteig, Germany, Herman Riefle runs a European Media Academy for radio, television, journalism, art and music. His academy's director is Dr. Paul McClendon from Tulsa. ERB's President, Bert Dorenbos also runs the Rainbow Family Channel which hopes to grow eventually into a twenty-four hour satellite network for both radio and television. Dorenbos's strategy is to evangelise Europe. Creating Christian media is not an aim in itself. "It is dependent on faithful programme-makers and Churches."

By the turn of the century it is likely that satellite communications will be as commonplace in the life of the European churches as they are already in Billy Graham's missions. But nowadays a satellite up-link dish still adds a touch of excitement and glamour. 'Bouncing Billy' was the excited headline in one British religious weekly, less concerned with the message than with the ultra-modern medium. Satellites may not be the angels of the endtimes but, long before they are even plugged in, they can greatly excite the faithful. In the parking lots of American hotels, the big dishes are sometimes illuminated. Any Southern Baptist megachurch that is worth its salt has a very large up-link dish which is always visible from the road. It stands where, in another religious tradition, a roadside crucifix once stood. The European marketing men who believe that SKY Television will attract another million customers just as soon as receiving dishes have been successfully miniaturised may be quite wrong. A dish beside the bedroom window may be one man's eyesore but it may be another man's status symbol. And some people will always like eyesores!

Quite apart from public-entertainment broadcasting, satellites have many applications that can be useful to the churches. In the United States, there are countless examples of information and teaching materials being distributed by satellite. A far more important body than its name may suggest, the Sunday School Board of the Southern Baptist Convention distributes material weekly to member churches across the country. In 1992, EPD, the highly professional press agency of the German Evangelical Church, will switch from radio-telex to satellite technology. Using the Olympus satellite, groups of European Christians are experimenting with distance-learning and video distribution. Olympus, the last of the L-Sats, was built for the European Space Agency by British Eurospace. About fifty groups are hoping to use Olympus before it expires. The groups all belong to Eurostep. It is an umbrella organisation with charitable and educational objectives. The ubiquitous Dave Adams is Vice-President.

Two religious groupings, *Skopos* and EON are particularly active. The *Skopos* contribution to Olympus schedule has included programmes on the Epistle to the Romans and the theology of Lesslie Newbiggin. EON stands for the Ecumenical Olympus Network. Its members come from most of the traditional churches and the greatest feather in the EON cap has been to organise the transmission of GENFEST, a major rally in Rome of the international *Foccolare* movement. The Olympus satellite is important because it provides a training area in an activity where positioning is all-important. Other possibilities exist on other satellites.

The Olympus output is not the kind of thing that made Tony Verna famous in the broadcasting world. An amazing variety of training videos follow one another through the programme schedules in a continuous *non sequitur*. The enthusiasts of Eurostep are displaying their wares. Each programme segment has absolutely no relationship whatever to the next. Nobody could possibly watch Olympus continuously. Someone might watch at a certain time (or set the VCR to 'download' in the middle of the night) if what is sought is one specific half-hour on Italian plastic surgery or Teach Yourself Turkish.

With support from the EEC, the European Institute for the Media at Manchester sponsors a different broadcasting experiment – Channel E on the very visible Astra. Channel E's potential audience is large. It can be received by every DBS viewer of Sky TV. The channel's first series of transmissions did not include religious programmes. In the orbiting years that remain to them, Olympus and perhaps Channel E, could do valuable work for the European Churches. If, for instance, there is a shortage of teachers in Christian communication subjects, seminaries across Europe – even Henry Tudor College! – could bridge the gap with distance-learning.

But Olympus has a further and rather important problem which highlights the wider European difficulty. In its DBS role, Olympus can transmit in either D-MAC or D2 MAC. But Britain's BSB company enjoys a monopoly of certain D-MAC receiving components (the 'chips'). This only leaves D2–MAC for Olympus's direct broadcast transmissions and, since there is no mass market for DBS in D2–MAC, European manufacturers have been reluctant to produce low-cost receivers. In other words, the satellite is in the sky, religious narrowcasters are organising themselves enthusiastically – but hardly anyone can watch!

Dave Adams is undaunted. "You can always change satellites. Over the next ten years, religious television will have to be addressed on a European level. Money's not the real problem. Technology's only half the problem. What the Churches have got to do is find out what they want to do and why. Christians have to find the will and, just as important, they have to come up with the ideas. At the moment, that's where the real shortage is."

CHAPTER 6

Revolutions per minute

There is no need to make a convoluted confession. The plot was simple. "If you don't know the answer to a question, don't reveal your ignorance by going into too much detail. Spend the whole three hours arguing that the question itself is logically flawed." This has nothing to do with one particular incident, still less with religious broadcasting. It is the general remembrance of an exam technique favoured by long-departed schoolmasters with Ancient Greek pretensions. To some of us, this became a survival technique, a weapon of last resort to see us through university and worse.

European Religious Broadcasting would be a sitting duck! The first happy hour could be spent arguing that, apart from a set of shared memories, Europe itself does not exist. Very few Europeans can agree about Europe. Perhaps this is because, as it is said in Poland, "Some of us know the price of being European while others have escaped the inheritance tax". The most difficult coconut to knock down would be religious. Most reasonable citizens tend to come up with a thoroughly straightforward definition. People know what they mean by 'religious' – even if they themselves are not. Perhaps we ought to spend no more than fifteen minutes on 'religious'. Indeed, we could make the case for a word change. In an increasingly multifaith Europe, the real need is to ask what we mean by 'Christian' programming. Without any doubt at all, we should save most of our ammunition for 'broadcasting'. This is a wildly imprecise concept and a word that no two people can agree about. Arguments rage at every level about the nature of broadcasting. The word has so many meanings that we could easily filibuster right up to the final bell. Rubbing the writer's cramp from our fingers, we can then leave the examination hall behind. "European Religious Broadcasting is indeed a meaningless expression and undeserving of serious attention! Q.E.D."

An alternative strategy, also favoured by Ancient Greeks, is to break things down into particular segments in order to cross-check those features that might be universal. This process has its own risks. Others may rightly argue that our arbitrary demarcation lines cause their own distortions and generalisations. So without claiming overmuch for the method, let us take a phrase of Pope John Paul II that "Europe has two lungs, East and West." When Christian broadcasting is compartmentalised, a common factor becomes apparent. In both halves of Europe, East and West, Christians in the broadcast media are facing change, confusion and revolution. But, to pursue the Polish Pope's analogy, lungs require air. And an increasing amount of the European religious atmosphere has been blown back across the Atlantic.

"Eastern Europe is a Klondike". The words belonged to the senior communications officer of one of the West European Churches. He was speaking in a committee room in ecumenical Geneva and he was unhappy. He was speaking not long before Rumania's first free elections for forty years. Prospectors are pouring into the former Socialist states. Among the gold-diggers are religious broadcasters, more concerned with striking it lucky than with serving the indigenous servants of God. Every conceivable religious operation is at work in the new democracies. Hari Krishna and the New Age movement are highly visible. A right-wing hero, Reverend Sun Myung Moon, founder of the Unification Church and much else, held an annual meeting of his World Media Association in a Moscow hotel. During his Russian tour, he exchanged elaborate verbal bouquets with Mr. Gorbachev. Reverend Moon, who once described Communism as "Satan's greatest weapon", told the President that the Soviet Union would play "a major role in the plan of God to construct a world of peace". In Hungary, the Mormons were active long before the last gasp of the Communist government. 'Success Theology' from Texas has reared its seductive head. Jehovah's Witnesses are not new arrivals. Having suffered persecution and denial of civil rights under both Fascist and Communist regimes, they are now free and gaining ground.

'Base camp' for most of these religious prospectors is not Western Europe but across the sea, in the continent where the original Klondike happened. The collapse of socialism in Eastern Europe has given something of a fillip to the battered army of North American TV preachers. They were already reeling from the financial aftershocks of the Bakker-Swaggart scandals, a fire that has been fed by something the President of NRB described as the "poured gasoline of the last three years". Jim Bakker and Jimmy Swaggart will go down in broadcasting history as the terrible twins whose sexual sins found them out. The whole world laughs when the gamekeeper is found to be a poacher after all. But it is neither right nor wise to laugh. Both Swaggart and Bakker are bizarre symptoms of an unhealthy system that was created not by any particular Televangelist nor even by a conspiracy of Televangelists. The North American Electronic Church was allowed to happen by nothing less than an agency of the United States government. A broadcasting environment has been formed in which, if the Swaggarts and Bakkers and Oral Robertses and Robert Schullers did not exist, it would be necessary to invent them.

Darwin would understand. The American government has created an ecological niche. Televangelists evolve inevitably and only the fittest survive. Swaggart and Bakker may diminish but, as they do so, newer and rising stars will move forward and take their place. This continual process of evolution which favours the entrepreneurial TV preacher, and which almost obliterated the mainline Churches from America's screens, emanates from the directives of the United States' own Federal Communications Commission. When, more than twenty years ago, a vital brick was dislodged, a whole edifice of publicly-accountable broadcasting came tumbling down.

The Federal Communications Commission directed that religious broadcasting would still be required on American screens but that, in future, this religious airtime could be *paid for*. Two spectacular results followed. Religious broadcasting almost immediately became big business. The nationally-known Televangelists have to spend enormous sums on airtime. In the year before he contested the Republican nomination, the preaching politician, Pat Robertson, had to find more than $220 million to buy time on 5,000 cable systems. The only people who can provide this money are the viewers themselves.

So the Televangelist has first of all to be an entertainer... in order to build up a big enough audience, in order to receive enough financial support to stay on air as an entertainer.

Amazingly, twenty-seven per cent of the Televangelists' donors are Roman Catholics. They seem to think that a garish gospel may be better than no gospel at all. Another result of the deregulation of religious broadcasting is equally visible. The Churches have been knocked from their privileged perch. They cannot take the heat of free-market competition. Catholics and Lutherans and Methodists have been all but banished from the box. There are no more Archbishop Fulton Sheens with their own advertisement-supported programmes.

By Western European standards, the American churches are packed to overflowing. There are more Catholics in the USA than there are Britons in Britain. There are more Southern Baptists than there are Dutch in Holland. But the Churches cannot cope with buying time. Nor can they afford to buy time. So despite Jimmy Swaggart and Jim Bakker and Oral Roberts, the show will go on.

LIGHT COMES FROM THE EAST

The spectacular events in Eastern Europe provided the Electronic Church with a modicum of new confidence or at the very least a new talking point. The 'possibility-thinking' Robert Schuller has been particularly visible both in Moscow itself and in Hungary. Most of the major television ministries are in some way involved. For the less scrupulous preachers, Eastern Europe, like Northern Ireland, has been nothing more than a photo opportunity. The preaching star, his wife and their camera crew make a very public journey. 'God's instrument' stays around just long enough to be filmed looking purposefully into the Danube and declaiming a word or two. Then he goes straight back to next week's show as fast as his private jet can travel – to the managed applause of his studio audience.

But this is the vulgar-most tip of the Electronic Church. Most members of National Religious Broadcasters are sincere enough. Some are born-again Christians who cut their broadcasting teeth in missionary radio. But, despite NRB's Conservative Evangelical basis, just about anyone who really wants to seems able to join. So despite the fine print of its statement of faith, NRB is really a trade association, a colourful coalition of Fundamentalists, Charismatics, Pro-Life and Family-values groups, Christian Zionists, Millenarians, Success-'n-Life ministries and Positive-Thinking Pelagians who would have given Martin Luther apoplexy. But the TV preachers, great and small, could not exist if they did not represent something real in America's cultural and class structure. Only a minority are scandalous or bizarre. Most run respectable religious businesses or thriving churches. There is a great deal of difference between the hundreds of folksy Church services that are broadcast each American Sunday and the glitzy mid-week religious talk shows. Nevertheless, three years before Timosoara, there was much serious talk throughout the whole Electronic Church of God's resurrection of Israel and of the coming Armageddon. The broadcast satellites in the sky might be nothing less than apocalyptic winged creatures foreseen by St. John.

But now there is a rosier tone. God has persuaded Pharaoh to let the ancient peoples go. Strong defence policies paid off. Free enterprise has been proved to be a better system. It enabled President Reagan to spend the Evil Empire to death – or, at least, to spend it to exhaustion and leave it slumped under the international poker table. So, this is no time to be talking too loudly about the end of the world. America can rejoice again in its European roots and repay its gospel debts to the lands of the Reformation. And in Eastern Europe the effect has been startling. Anybody who is anybody in American religious broadcasting has been doing the grand tour. In the first five months of 1990 one Pentecostal pastor in Budapest, Pastor Louis Simonfalvi, received representatives from no less than nine American media groups. According to the pastor, each visiting ministry wanted to "carve out its own empire". When Pastor Simonfalvi spoke of the media needs and plans of his own Church, there was 'no positive response'.

But there is, of course, another side to the coin. The European Reformation created national Churches from which many Evangelicals have long felt excluded. From the time of the Pilgrim Fathers, they have dreamed of a godly Protestant land across the sea where the Erastian errors of the Reformation have been cured and there is no state religion. The United States is almost viewed as a protecting power. "Come over to Macedonia and help us." Billy Graham and Luis Palau have been enthusiastically received. Indeed a two-hour recording of Billy Graham's Budapest crusade was carried on Hungarian TV. Some high-profile religious events clearly encourage native Christians and do not simply massage the folks back home. And, of course, Western Churches are entitled to take a legitimate interest. The Bible Societies of many countries have been particularly successful in meeting real needs. Not all the broadcasting ministries have been self-seeking. A hundred Protestant organisations have European offices. Long before the invention of *perestroika*, the Toronto-based Christian broadcaster David Mainse had a special concern for Europe, East and West. About one hundred European producers, technicians and presenters have served their apprenticeship on Mainse's well-regarded *One Hundred Huntley Street* programme. The United States has massive numbers of first- and second-generation exiles. Many religious broadcasters, including the mainline VISN Interfaith Network, feel that they would win audiences if they could remind American viewers of their East European origins.

The College of Communication of Televangelist Pat Robertson's Regent Universtity in Virginia provides educational assistance to Eastern Europe. The University now gives several full scholarships but many would-be students have neither the educational background nor the time to attend a full-time course in the United States. Other avenues are being explored. One initiative was a 1990 leadership conference, co-hosted by Regent University and the *Evandeoski Teoloski Fakultet* at Osijek, Yugoslavia. Sessions included the 'Biblical Basis for Mass Communication' and 'Identifying and exploiting small business opportunities'. There followed a two-day meeting in Munich with business and Church leaders to discuss the need for an Evangelical university in Europe which would provide communication training. Says Dr. David Clark, the Dean of Regent's College of Communication, "Doing a Regent University in Europe is not our goal. We would like to be facilitators and help to create an institution with a thoroughly biblical worldview". It is likely that the new university will be sited in "close proximity to what we used to think of as Eastern Europe".

The media missionaries from the West have a variety of motives. As for the East European Churches themselves, they are often confused and poorly structured. Some are still tarred by the political sins of their grandfathers. In most countries, the traditional churches need time to recover from the nightmare. But the problem is that there is no time. Four decades of anti-religious propaganda has had its effect. Dr. Lukacs Lazlo of the Hungarian Catholic Church speaks of fifteen years of dictatorship which was then followed by a "soft dictatorship under a surface of warm words" when everyone had at least to "appear a Marxist". Western-style consumerism is hardly the best environment for a recovery of faith. Suddenly, every citizen has a right to publish his own beliefs. A Church of heroes now faces a fourfold problem of "lack of experience", "lack of experts", "lack of resources" and "lack of appropriate structures and functions". The new freedoms cannot alter the fact that the idea of public dialogue has been extinguished. "And this has happened not least within the Church itself," says Dr. Lazlo.

There is an acute shortage of leaders. Many are old and a few, for a special reason, are reluctant. For years, many monks in Eastern Europe have had to live out their lives as train drivers or railway engineers or window cleaners. Some have never lived in a monastery. Who can blame them if they now want to begin to taste their special community vocation? Among Protestants, Orthodox and Catholics alike, some leaders were discredited in the eyes of the people. While the world moved forward, others survived by clinging fiercely to pre-war memories and customs. These leaders now find it hard to accept liturgical revisions, let alone the compromises that are necessary for television. There is a widespread need for new leadership and training materials. Within four months of the downfall of the Ceausescus, Walter Kast, a Swiss official with Campus Crusade for Christ, drove to Timosoara with equipment for test reception of the Olympus satellite. Picture quality was excellent and Kast believed that a new way was open to deliver training videos. Two days later, for commercial reasons, the beam was shifted westwards away from Rumania and the picture broke up!

The communication needs of the Eastern Churches are myriad. According to a Catholic spokesman, Latvian Television is being invaded by pornography and violence. The republic has a particular need for the training of journalists. Far to the South, a Yugoslavian priest says that: "From the East we have inherited atheism, while from the West we have received materialism. We now have the worst of both worlds." A Lithuanian communicator, Father Virginius Veilantas believes that it has been "relatively easy to get rid of Marxism but the problem is what to put in its place". He believes that more "East-East contact" is what is needed. This point is echoed in some Western ecumenical circles. As a sign of the times, the Council of European Churches (CEC), hoped to hold a consultation of its Soviet members in Tbilisi, Georgia. Unfortunately the Soviet Churches can only reserve hotel block-bookings with Western currency. In view of the complexity of the situation in the East, the Communications Department of the Lutheran World Federation (like CEC, a Geneva-based organisation) has turned its back on grand or global solutions. Help to Eastern communicators is now being targeted. It is being offered solely on a country-by-country basis.

The Eastern churches themselves must now take hard decisions about media priorites. If serious journalism has to be based on the written word, then small-scale newspapers may be a more urgent priority than expensive Western-style broadcasting. Apart from Poland, where the cohesion of Roman Catholicism has long rivalled that of the Party and where there have been a large number of vocations to the priesthood, most Eastern churches remain shell-shocked and poorly resourced. But nothing can alter the fact that significant broadcasting opportunities are opening up. In Poland the provisions for government censorship remain valid but are, of course, no longer applied. Poles are repairing their room in the new European home and, says Andrzej Drawicz, Chairman of Polish Radio and Television, "there will hopefully be room for a modest TV set". Democratisation of the mass media will mean that private broadcasting will soon be permitted, without creating (in Dr. Drawicz's words) "an all-levelling commercialism". He believes that Poland's attempt to strike such a balance may be useful to West Europeans. "We may prove useful to you."

Not too long ago, in most of Eastern Europe, religious broadcasting was only available on Radio Liberty, Vatican Radio, Voice of America and the other short-wave stations. Now, in their own cities, Christians can sit in the studios where, not long ago, religion was derided. Some clergy feel that they may have been handed a lightly-poisoned chalice. There is an understandable tradition in the East, nurtured by years of propaganda, of not believing in good news of any kind. Nevertheless, the state-owned broadcasting systems have acquired a new independence and credibility. New commercial systems are being established and cable already exists in a few places. For the first time since the Great Patriotic War, black-robed archbishops talk politics on Soviet programmes. The Christian children's video *Superbook* has been given a Russian dubbing by Soviet TV. Christmas carols ring out from Bucharest. East German pastors, megastars in the heady days of revolt, readjust themselves to a more prosaic media role. Hardly surprisingly, from the Baltic to the Black Sea, there is a tremendous variation in the access enjoyed by the Churches.

In Estonia, clergy of the re-invigorated Lutheran Church have been almost run off their feet by interviews about religion and nation-building. Long before the communicative Mr. Yeltsin became his Federation President, one Russian archbishop had organised his own Russian/English press service. A media spokesman for Slovenia's Catholics detects "a certain neutral role" on the part of state radio and television. He says, reluctantly, "We must use public radio for a couple of years yet." Pastor Simonfalvi, on the other hand, does not want to go into Hungarian studios if it means "being controlled by atheists". Great numbers of bilateral links and training arrangements are having some effect. East German Lutheran bishops have been given TV-interview training courses and equipped with radio telephones to improve their own day-to-day communication. A broadcasting specialist of one Eastern European Church laments the cautious camerawork that is used for the new broadcasts of the mass. "Who wants to look at the back of my bishop's neck for half an hour?" asks the frustrated cleric. On the other hand, when the West German Lutheran Church encouraged the ARD network to broadcast a live Pentecost Communion Service from Riga, a considerable training programme was also provided for Latvian broadcasters.

Throughout the former Eastern bloc and as a sign of the new constitutionalism, the Churches are being given airtime on the Western pattern. GDR Television has created a brand-new Religious Programmes Department. The Director is Volker von der Heydt, former TV commissioner for his country's Federation of Evangelical Churches. Polish Television has provided a number of twenty-minute religious slots. The Hungarian quota on state television is 3,000 minutes per year. Of these, 2,000 minutes are for Roman Catholics. The remaining 1,000 minutes are shared out between Protestants and the non-Christian sects. Radio frequencies are in great demand. In Budapest, seventy groups are waiting for their own space on the airwaves. The problem for Christian communicators – Orthodox, Lutheran, Catholic and Reformed – is that they are ill-equipped and ill-trained. They are unable to respond to all the new opportunities and in many cases to fill to professional standards the airtime that is becoming increasingly available. Others wait in the wings, well-financed and only too willing to step into the ecclesiastical shoes. And overhead Western satellites are already beaming down everything from soft pornography to the so-called Worldwide Church of God.

Czechoslovakia, Hungary, Poland and the USSR have immense film-making talent and experience and as far as entertainment television and animation-work is concerned, their studios are likely to grow as low-wage producers for the rest of Europe. According to the British trade union leader, Alan Sapper, they will be the "Hong Kong" of Europe. Sadly, the short-term outlook is poor for authentic Eastern religious broadcasting. This is a tragedy for the whole continent for, of all the Christians of Europe, it is the Eastern Churches who have the most to say and teach. Most of them will be unable to muster the energy or resources to sound much of a counterblast to a blitz of Western influences, secular and religious.

But a minority of Christians have cheerfully adapted to the new realities. Church-builders in Leningrad now look to the United States for funds. In the city of Shostakovich and the Great Siege, glossy brochures announce a new megachurch. No doubt what it lacks in icons and onion domes will be more than made up for by a conspicuous satellite dish. Of course, this could be seen as just another continuation of the Leningrad tradition. After all, Peter the Great founded his city to be a window on the West. But now is the time for Christian Slavs and Magyars to look to their own twinkling lights – lights that have never been put out, even by Adolf Hitler or Joseph Stalin. From Dietrich Bonhoeffer to Vaclav Havel, Eastern Christians have shone like candles in a deep darkness. Now that the long night is over, these rather-disorganised, sometimes-compromised, long-derided, frequently-martyred, often-quarrelling, New Testament Christians have no more need to communicate by candlelight. If their media work is to make the necessary time-leap from 1939, they will need some Western equipment, expertise and careful training. But it would be ironic indeed if the flickering lights, which have survived the horrors of Heydrich, Rakosi and Ccasescu, cannot now be seen against the dazzle of entertainment television.

Ex Oriente Lux!

DIVERTING THE MAINSTREAM

Christian broadcasters in Western Europe are living through their own revolutions. This ought to come as no great surprise. Public broadcasting can never be static. It always has to make some response to new situations and changing public attitudes. So it is always mistaken to try to look back in time to some perceived Golden Age of broadcasting when everyone knew their place and Christianity was accorded its rightful place of honour on the airwaves. Ultimately the success of religious broadcasting will depend entirely on public interest. The Churches' fortunes may wax and wane. They may try to rely on an inevitable time-delay but in the end there is no escape from the facts of life and these will have to be reflected by broadcasters – even public-service broadcasters.

One of the more recent discoveries about broadcasting is that it cannot work miracles, whether in politics or religion. Broadcasting can reinforce attitudes and prejudices. It can quicken interest in those who are already interested. So throughout the seventy-year history of European broadcasting, the religious component has had to bear some relation to the place of religion in society. Perhaps in the 1920s Christianity was given too important a place on the airwaves. Or, rather, it was given a position that it could not later justify or defend. In the early years it was easier for the Churches to exercise power over the media because the leaders of the Churches still had great power in the land. Also they had played a prominent part in the formation of the new broadcasting services and of the influential religious advisory committees. But the hard fact remains. In situations where religion is not an important part of everyday life, religious broadcasting will be difficult.

Northern Ireland's polarised but highly religious situation provides the clearest example in all of Western Europe. *Sunday Sequence* is broadcast on BBC Radio Ulster on Sunday mornings. The first part of the programme is a religious magazine. This leads into the morning service, hence the 'sequence'. Very similar programme formats can be found on dozens of European radio stations. But by every standard of audience measurement, *Sunday Sequence* is an exceptionally successful programme. Listeners come from every section of Northern Ireland's divided population. It is regularly listened to by most political and religious leaders. The simple reason for its continuing success in the ratings is not its journalistic scoops nor even its objectivity nor the important regional role of BBC Radio Ulster. It is the simple fact that religion is an all-important subject to a large listening audience.

Northern Ireland is unique. As for the rest of North-West Europe, it became apparent fifty years ago that perhaps broadcasting itself had taken over the position that the Church itself had manifestly lost. Could it be that popular broadcasting had become the anointed heir to the medieval Church? Everyone with a receiver would have his own place in the new dispensation. North of the Alps the Churches were only parts of the secular *oikumene*. There is no longer a universal Church – only some widely-shared Christian values and, of course, the denominations which, by definition, are only segments of the listening congregations. A bishop of the Church of England sums up a sad state of affairs, "Christianity was our culture but now it is one of our choices".

In country after country the same story was repeated. Sooner or later religious broadcasting was considered too sensitive or too boring to be left to the Churches. It was yet another long-delayed triumph for sixteenth-century Erastianism. In the new nation-states of Europe, it was the bishop who had to take instructions from the civil power. Britain's original Defender of the Faith would have approved heartily of at least one of John Reith's pronouncements at the BBC: "Christianity happens to be the stated and official religion of this country; it is recognised by the crown." But King Henry would have certainly disapproved of another aspiration of the Director General. Reith wanted religious broadcasting which was "unassociated with any particular creed or denomination".

So the continuing problem for Christian broadcasting has been to cope with the fact that there is no single faith-group that can speak for all. In Britain, John Reith thought he knew the answer. He wanted programmes that would be fundamental, manly, uncontroversial, optimistic and non-denominational (and therefore Protestant?). Before long, a concept of mainstream religion began to be talked about. For advice about the meaning of 'mainstream', the BBC looked to the experts of the Sunday Committee (later CRAC) which was (of course!) made up of self-declared mainstream institutions. But, as the years have gone by, the mainstream has widened considerably. Nevertheless, Unitarians had great problems launching out into the stream. Jews on the other hand (and are they not unitarians too?) were readily accepted. In multifaith Britain, Moslems and Hindus are now offered a place within the religious broadcasting mainstream but Mormons and Jehovah's Witnesses are not. Most of Europe's national broadcasting corporations operate their own rules of thumb. In Sweden, Christians who *could* join the World Council of Churches (and this, of course, is a wider group than those who in fact *have* joined) are welcome to broadcast.

But the religious mix varies greatly. Each country has found its own way of defining the limits of religious pluralism. In Italy, the Roman Catholic Church has no special need for concordats or formal agreements. The broadcasting institutions of the Italian state know exactly where they stand in relation to the church. Even to most non-believers, a Pope is a superstar with all the glamour of a modern monarch. To be a 'vaticanist' is a skilled, full-time and honourable occupation in the Italian media. Curiously, the overwhelming presence of the Bishop of Rome has resulted in a unique broadcasting freedom for Italy's Protestant minorities. They were given their first programme slot by a non-Catholic general of the American Fifth Army. Perhaps because there is a surfeit of vaticanists but a shortage of ecumenists in public broadcasting, the Protestant Churches have been left to their own devices. They seem to have a *carte blanche* from RAI for the production of their own weekly half-hour television programme.

In the Catholic South, the Spanish and Portuguese Churches have concentrated resources on their own wholly-owned broadcasting networks. Portugal's *Ràdio Renascença* takes scrupulous care to ensure that its advertising department is fully detached. In the

71

Protestant North, the folk Churches of the Reformation still enjoy an absolute majority. In the Lutheran tradition, the link with state broadcasting is very close. Among the Nordic Churches, only the Finns insist on producing their own broadcasts of religious services. Throughout Scandinavia and Finland, the church attendance statistics are disappointing but figures for baptisms, marriages and funerals are still spectacular. Ninety-six per cent of all Icelanders are baptised. The *Andakt* is a typically-Norse reflection on the meaning of life. Although they can sometimes last for as long as ten or even fifteen minutes, *Andakter* are liberally scattered throughout the quieter byways of public radio and television.

In the Netherlands, in many ways the home of European radio, religious broadcasting was built on the fact that Dutch society is 'pillared'. Catholic and Protestant broadcasting associations share airtime, and a proportion of the licence fee, according to the number of their paid-up members. In egalitarian France, broadcasting by Catholics, Orthodox, Protestants, Jews and Moslems is now confined to Sunday mornings. There is a special sequence of religious programmes on *Antenne 2*, the second of France's six major channels. Religious organisations, including the (Catholic) *Comité Français de Radio-Télévision* and *Présence Protestante* now have to pay towards the high cost of airtime. The annual Catholic broadcasting budget is F.Fr 20 million and most of it is required for their weekly flagship programme, *Le Jour du Seigneur*. Eighty per cent is raised from 125,000 Catholic subscribers who are approached through *les mailings*.

In Germany on the other hand, the Protestant and Catholic Churches have a constitutional place in broadcasting and its decision-making. West German public broadcasting is so highly regionalised that, when it comes to broadcasting, most German regional governments do not accept the Treaty of Rome. The Churches have commissioners to the regional broadcasting stations. The two established Churches also have impressive and centralised communication structures. Each Church's media directorate enjoys a considerable power in the publicly-owned media. The communications department of the German Evangelical Church is also mandated to speak for the Free Churches. No changes are envisaged for public-service religious broadcasting but there are now some difficulties with programme scheduling.

72

Many of the traditional Churches of Western Europe still enjoy a privileged position in national broadcasting, and they do not pay for it. Long before Marconi, each country reached its separate accommodation with its religious institutions. After the Reformation, countries were either Catholic or Protestant or, in the case of the German states, *Cuius regio, eius religio* (Whatever is the prince's religion will be the religion of his principality). But religious mainstreams soon proved increasingly difficult to chart. Much of the history of Europe and its colonies has been concerned with the struggle of people to be included within the mainstream. Europe is now a continent of many faiths and of none. New currents in the stream include humanism, secularism and atheism as well as Christianity and other faiths.

For fifty years, the mainstream Churches have enjoyed a special and somewhat privileged relationship with the national corporations. In the United States, a broadly-similar linkage was nicknamed 'the sweetheart deal'. But the problem now, for West European broadcasters and churchmen alike, is that public-service broadcasting (and this can be supported by advertising as well as taxation) is facing the heat of new competition. In order to survive and to justify their continued subsidy from the public purse, publicly-owned channels have to retain an audience. In a protected environment, free from rivals and predators, programmes can be made on almost any basis. Broadcasters can set themselves all manner of noble tasks from the protection of cultural diversity to the preservation of regional dialects. But nowadays public-service channels also have to respond to the demands of the marketplace – or, at least, they too have to be seen to retain a market share. The concept of broadcasting is itself in question. More choice must lead inevitably to less *broad*casting and more *narrow*casting. In other words, channels have to become increasingly generic. They will provide specialities; music videos, data, game shows, natural history, children's programmes, sport, films, news – and religion?

The only way in which religious programmes can now remain on prime-time public television is when audience figures provide their own justification or by private treaty between competing channels. Increasingly, public-service obligations are being discharged by confining religious programmes to secondary channels. In other words, religious broadcasting is no longer on display in the front window of the shop. It is still in the store, but now it has to be looked for. In many countries, religious programmes have been removed completely from the main entertainment television channel. Since it was made commercial, France's TF1 has forged ahead in the ratings. It has attracted a continuous stream of talent from its publicly-funded competitors. TF1's news broadcasts dominate the market. However it transmits no religious programmes, apart from occasional 'specials'. The same is true in most of Scandinavia where there is a rather impressive range of religious programmes – church services, *Andakter*, 'views of life' and programmes of spiritual songs and music. As it is in France, Northern religion is a second-channel speciality.

So, to combine three maritime metaphors, have the Churches nailed their colours to the mast of a sinking ship – or a ship that is now being converted to steam? Perhaps they have. The revolution in West European broadcasting will claim many casualties. Ten years ago a senior British broadcasting executive lamented that "the last chapter in the institutional history of broadcasting has begun". He was premature but he may not have been wrong. But the idea that the airwaves are a public trust and not simply another marketable commodity has many friends within the mainstream Churches. "You cannot hold me responsible for everything you see on KRO," said the late Cardinal Alfrink to an irate Dutch viewer. And in other ways, the stand-off between public-service broadcasting and the Churches has great value. "The Churches would need a one-line motive for broadcasting," says a British broadcaster, Andrew Barr. "I don't need a motive except simply to serve the viewer."

It can be argued that public service is, in any case, a deeply religious concept and ideally suited to reflect the religious traditions of a community. Even its most obvious fault – the tendency to steer down the middle of most roads and to settle for a liberal consensus – can often be cured. Preaching is not necesarily impossible on well-regulated stations and souls can be saved. Evangelical Christians do not have to be excluded and, to be fair, many have excluded themselves by their inability to understand the medium. Religious certainties can be aired in public-service broadcasting, as well as religious doubts. Advertisement-support does not have to cause an insuperable ideological problem. Public-service Christian broadcasting does not have to be reduced to a broad, inclusive religiosity that does nothing much but span the mainstream. Nor is there a law of the Medes and Persians that says that programmes have to be phenomenological; that they have to be *about* religion rather than *religious*.

Good service has been given to the Churches – and sometimes a better service than the Churches have deserved. But the trend is unlikely to be reversed. This is not to say that Europe has necessarily seen the last of media monopolies. The tendency for media power to be concentrated in a few hands is more apparent than ever. But the *national* monopolies have been broken. Just as terrestrial broadcasting is having to co-exist with different delivery systems, so the old government broadcasting corporations have had to face up to competition. The older pattern of financing, by various forms of taxation or subscription, is hardly capable of sustaining existing broadcasting commitments, let alone providing for an expansion of services. Whether the Churches like it or not, their allies in public-service broadcasting have less and less to offer in the 'sweetheart deal'. Every year, more and more choice is being offered to the broadcasting consumer. With the growth of the video market, broadcasters are not even assured of the undivided attention of each domestic TV set. A more competitive commercial environment means that channels will require a greater specialisation and self-determination. There will be fiercer competition for a finite reserve of advertisement income and for an increasingly fragmented audience. There will be less and less time for religion.

But this is not the whole story. A free-market philosophy would not itself be enough to bring about this revolution in Western Europe's broadcasting. Without a technological revolution, the rapid increase in the number of broadcast channels would have been impossible. Despite its grandiloquent name, terrestrial broadcasting means nothing more than to transmit from an aerial that is ultimately attached to *terra firma* rather than one that is fixed to an orbiting satellite. For most of the next ten years, this original, traditional and, more often than not, national form of broadcasting will continue to be the main delivery system for Western Europe's television programmes. However, in many countries, the system's days are numbered. By the end of the decade, and with the great exception of France, the main delivery system for domestic television could well be satellite-to-cable-to-home. By the year 2,000, the continent's terrestrial broadcasting could be increasingly confined to Europe's thousands of radio stations. In any case, there will have been a massive increase in the quantity of broadcasting outlets and, it seems, of new media opportunities for Christian broadcasters. The linkage between the technological revolution and Western Europe's so-called broadcast deregulation is complex. Technological changes are making many new channels available. At the same time (but even faster) free-market ideas have triumphed throughout Europe, and broadcasting products, including religious products, will have to take their chances in an increasingly competitive marketplace.

The market has arrived and the religious mainstream is ever-wider. But not everything on the landscape has changed since the days of Reith. Religious worship is still broadcast by most national networks. What is different is the justification for these programmes and perhaps this difference is a true measure of the broadcasting revolution. The best defence for the inclusion of broadcast worship in programme schedules is no longer the value of religion to society as a whole. Now, it is consumer demand from a still-sizeable religious audience segment. "If religion is for a minority, then so is football," says Ernest Rea, the BBC's Head of Religious Broadcasting. And he points out that the audience for the *Daily Service* on BBC Radio 4 is higher now than at any time since the 1960s. The refreshing truth that has been finally revealed by Western Europe's broadcasting revolution may simply be this: religious broadcasting cannot work miracles. Not unreasonably, it has to depend ultimately on religion's value to the community. *Cuius religio, eius radio.*

CHAPTER 7

Neil Postman and others:

Pierre Babin, Ingmar Lindqvist, Franco Lever, David Holloway and Cardinal Carlo Maria Martini

In his book *The Image*, Daniel Boorstin doubts that photography has given us a new language. Boorstin makes a point that Aristotle would have certainly made too. No matter how wide-angle the lens, a single photograph – a seascape perhaps – can never convey the same meaning as the spoken word 'Sea'. With our written and spoken language, we have the possibility, in one three-letter word, to include every ocean on the face of the earth. With a camera we record nothing more than what is in front of us. We freeze a portion of reality. It follows that not all media have the same possibilities. Computers linked by modems can share far more than native Americans joined by smoke signals. So in this chapter at least, our opening photographic theme will be laid aside! The better communicators are words.

Communication, like politics, is the art of the possible. It has been said many times that the 1990s will present the Christian communicators of Europe with new opportunities and possibilities. But possibility can be used carelessly. The facts are obvious to all; technology is changing, frontiers are coming down and regulations are being liberalised. But are these revolutions enough to create possibility? Most Christians have no doubt at all. Broadcasting is there to be used. A television set is simply inanimate – "lights, wires and a vacuum-filled tube" – or so European Religious Broadcasters were told at their 1990 meeting. And too few would argue.

But especially now, the Churches have to begin looking beneath the obvious. Open studio doors are not enough. They may look inviting, especially to highly-motivated people who have, up-to-now, felt excluded. But inconvenient though it may seem, the question has to be asked until it is answered: "What, in fact, is *possible* for Christians in broadcasting?" Even the most casual reader of the New Testament could not fail to notice that communication is central. The whole point of the Christ-event has to be God's communication with man. This, in turn, leaves Christian men and women with a communication imperative. There is no option but for Christians to live communicating lives – with God and with each other. But does it then follow that every means of communication possesses the same possibility? Can the gospel be communicated by photograph, by computer, by smoke signal or even by television?

In *Amusing Ourselves to Death*, Neil Postman questions the possibility of television doing anything useful for the community, let alone for the gospel. Postman makes elegant contrasts between the expectations of George Orwell and Aldous Huxley. In *1984* and *Animal Farm*, Orwell foresaw a world where loudspeakers and thought machines would regiment the masses. The media would be instruments of totalitarian control. But in Huxley's *Brave New World*, humanity would control itself by its longing for pleasure, comfort and satisfaction. *Amusing Ourselves to Death*, has been described as a devastating indictment of American television. It comes down firmly on the side of Huxley.

Is Postman, who claims to stand in the developing tradition of Marshall McLuhan, a media prophet? Or is he only a beguiling and amusing cynic? He laments the passing of the 'typographical age'. There is nothing in the US Constitution on the subject but, because of television, a fat man cannot now be his country's President. Postman congratulates God on promulgating the second commandment. Graven images are a clear danger. At least the Almighty was wise enough to foresee the connection between forms of communication and the quality of culture. To Postman, the problem is not *what* people watch on television. It is *that* they watch at all. And there is no escape. So many people watch television that even the non-watchers, like non-smokers perhaps, inhale from other people. Whatever happens, television must *not* be asked to improve. Heaven forbid! That would only make things more difficult. Television must get *worse!* Television can only amuse. When it pretends to have serious, high-falutin cultural aspirations, it is really dangerous.

Postman does not go quite so far as does the euphoniously-named Jerry Mander in his *Four Arguments for the Elimination of Television*. Postman sees television feeding on context-free information. Unless today is Budget Day, nothing that we see on tonight's television news will impinge even slightly on our own lives. The average length of a television news shot is three and a half seconds. The world is buried under its new communication networks but nothing serious is being said. What is the value of flashing the news round the world that a princess has whooping cough? A little limply perhaps, Postman concludes with a page or two that puts forward media education as society's only hope for a cure.

Amusing Ourselves to Death deserves the attention of all religious broadcasters, for Postman does not stand alone but in the vanguard of a very large army of American academics. For the present, Europeans are asking fewer awkward questions. They are increasingly concerned with quality, which is the pivot point for most of the political arguments about radio and television. In many European countries, highly-motivated volunteers, who are concerned for society's moral standards, monitor the output of public broadcasting. In Britain Mary Whitehouse has become a household name. For many years, KKL in Oslo provided a monitoring service for Norwegian MPs. Throughout Italy, there are many parish film centres, where members of the congregation are encouraged to pass a judgment on what they have been watching.

To Postman, the question of content would be a red herring. He does not say if he objects to televised pornography but he certainly prefers TV that is undeniable rubbish. He asks, and answers to his own satisfaction at least, some fundamental questions about the medium. On the whole European Christians are not greatly concerned with these questions. Europeans are talking a great deal about communication, technological breakthroughs, new channels and new evangelistic opportunities, especially in Eastern Europe. Some Christians, who have been long excluded from the mainstream, are preparing eagerly to get afloat. But the urge to communicate is not enough. One does not have to be a fervent disciple of Postman to know that a television set may be more than "lights, wires and a vacuum-filled tube". Nor must fundamental questions always result in negative answers. Far from it. Several Europeans who are occupied in pondering the meaning of television have arrived at answers that leave them so profoundly positive that, compared with Neil Postman, they are far away at the other end of the rainbow. For the remainder of this chapter, they will put their case, not in well-marshalled *written* arguments but through brief excerpts of reported speech.

Père Pierre Babin, a French priest, educator and communicator and a former collaborator with Marshall McLuhan, is the Director of the CREC-AVEX media centre in Lyon.

Christianity is not only a doctrine and a dogma. It's fundamentally a covenant, *une alliance*.

To express this covenant, we need stories, games, music, songs, affective expression, miracles. These are more important than dogma. Dogma comes after.

TV is bad sometimes. I agree. But the Spirit is greater. What is essential is not dogma or theory but communication. You communicate more through stories and playing. And why not?

Some people reduce Christianity until it is only understood by scholars. They make a confusion between spirituality and thinking. The centre of thinking is not a school... It is a meal. Christ first shared bread and wine. The centre of communication is not a communication of ideas but of body.

This is my body. In TV, you can say 'This is my body' better than in a catechism. TV is not to give a lecture but to express who you are. The medium of TV is ideal. First of all, it is *image* and that is much better than a book.

But the Bible is a book.

The Bible *became* a book. The book was first of all a community. With the printing press, the book became individualised.

Today theologians can't express the Bible. Evangelists are best.

80

But surely TV is a disembodied medium?

How can you say that! When I look at you, I see only an image. The privilege of TV is to – how do you say it – *sculpt* a body. In TV you accentuate a kind of immediacy. You accentuate the effect of presence. Also the voice. You accentuate the imagination.

Do you know the Minitel? It's our interactive keyboard service from French Telecom. Here in France, a lot of people are making love using their Minitel.

But surely it can't be real love?

What is real? Person-to-person can be stronger by telephone. Physical presence could be stronger with TV than with a teacher teaching fifty students. We have a TV presenter here in France. Some people kiss her on the screen.

But it's not one-to-one.

In TV, you are one-to-one one-way! There's a bishop in Brazil. He impressed me. He changed my way of thinking – by TV.

Even feedback is possible in a rudimentary kind of way. People learn when their programmes are failing.

What do you do at CREC-AVEX?

We are a centre for formation. Students study the theory of creation. Usually they already have doctrines which they then illustrate. That's not correct. At CREC-AVEX, we go from *experience* to *expression*. We put experience before creation.

You have spoken a good deal about modulation. What is it?

Modulation? Modulation is a complex of vibrations. The essence of this (TV) language is modulation – an effect on your sensorial system. It can make you calm. Colour can affect your unconscious system. We have known about lullabies for centuries. That's the new capacity – to express the message of God through the specific quality of modulation.

Is TV better than the real thing?

TV is not better! I can't use those words better or worse! TV is different! We have to discover the specific qualities of TV and then link them to special aspects of the Church.

What are they?

Not catechism or doctrine but the things that affect people, their imagination, their beliefs, their hearts. You have to find these aspects in the message of Christ. TV is best when it provokes miracles. That is why the Charismatics are so good at TV. There's a theology of miracles and we must think a lot about it.

What kind of miracles?

Think of that poor lonely lady. With TV you can break her solitude. *Fortunately* she has TV. If your presence – in TV – is full of inner life, you produce an effect.

The Church must represent the paradise of Christ through TV. Some say TV is entertainment – pleasure. Okay! Why not? If TV can express the paradise of Christ, I think it can bring more life.

*

Ingmar Lindqvist is Finnish. He is a philosopher and writer and produces religious television programmes for Finland's Swedish-speaking minority. In the wide spectrum of communication ideologies, Dr. Lindqvist stands rather nearer to Neil Postman than to Pierre Babin, but a long way from both.

If you want to maximise your audience, TV forces you to be conservative. You must talk to people the way they want to be talked to. Talk in new ways and you're out! Commercial interests force you to be conservative – to keep entertaining the audience.

The American Televangelists have realised what successful TV is all about. They produce religion in the form of conservative entertainment – if it is religion.

What do you mean by communication?

When we talk about communication, we talk about our efforts to make reality visible.

I think of three aspects – not necessarily equal. They are meditation, information, communication.

Meditation is when I make reality visible to myself – when I see where I am. And this can happen even when I am talking to people.

Information is when I tell people what I have found out about reality.

Communication is when we try to make reality visible in a joint effort.

Information is one-way communication. If you do not allow others to question you, communication is reduced and restricted to information, to *communicatio interrupta*. I am telling you in order to change you. I know. You don't.

This is the only way for Fundamentalists – to change people to the way you think. It's the way of dictators. We see much of it in our Churches. Liturgies, and even Church buildings, are built to inform. Pulpits are up in the air. Everything is built around seeing the 'one who knows' – the one who has information from above.

The mass media are geared to information – to one-way communication. The journalist is the one who made it. *Product* is what it is.

Fundamentalists think they have the product. If faith is something you *know*, then you have it.

It's not simply a question of *using* media. It's a matter of what you think about faith. Once you think *faith* is the same as *knowing*, then you have no problem using the information media. Once you have the truth, it's no use discussing any more. Those that disagree with you are wrong. The Fundamentalist sees the mass media as God's greatest blessing to mankind. Not surprisingly, the communications satellites turn out to be his angels.

Where does this leave Communication Studies?

What normally has been labelled Communication Studies has pre-supposed that there is something *outside* communication. Communication is seen as a means of wrapping a message in the most suitable way. Then it can be unwrapped in unblemished condition. American scholars especially have been primarily concerned with the transportation of messages – not so much with the joint search for reality and meaning.

If you accept the idea that the only kind of reality we have access to is communicated reality, you are bound to communicate in a different way. So when you provide information, you do so to make communication possible.

I want to rescue that word communication for two-way communication. Communication, of course, has to do with community, communion, having in common. I want a chance to influence in both ways – so that together we can define reality.

Communication is never just a way of making reality as such visible but a way of defining reality. Every tradition in the world does this and we are defined by this.

In the beginning, there was just one reality definition – God's. What was needed to bring about the fall of Adam and Eve was just one deviant definition. Once you have *two* different definitions, then you have to choose. Fundamentalists still hope for paradise – for just one reality definition. They see it as their task to make everybody see reality the same way and to create total consensus.

But today competing definitions abound. Paradise *is* lost. We can't just inform. We have to choose – choose the truth we want to live by. Faith is not faith if we just inform.

What then can we do?

I am searching for a way between nihilism and fundamentalism. That is also the way of Jesus, I think.

The Fundamentalists, once they have the truth, cannot lose it. They have to hang on to it. So truth becomes a prison. If you question their truth, you have not realised it is the truth you question!

Plato said "Once you know what is good, you cannot but do good". According to Marx, there is no return from the classless society once you have reached it. Fundamentalists try to wring your truth from you and imprison you in their absolute truth.

Jesus had a rather different way of looking at truth. 'The truth shall make you free' – free from all final reality definitions, free to keep searching, free to communicate and free to find communal and individual meaning.

My search is for a communicative society. I hate the connotations of an information society. To me that is a society where knowledge is power, because it is pre-supposed that it is possible to know for sure. It is a society crowded with consultants. They know!

What is the job of the Church in all this?

The church must maximise personal communication in the future. If faith is no finished product, our task cannot be to hand out finished products via the media. We should make programmes that make people talk to each other.

Radio is a good medium. It leaves me room. TV is more problematic and more challenging. The question is 'Can we promote communicative communication via TV?'

Postman makes negative definitions of entertainment. There are positive possibilities in entertainment, if you define entertainment as what turns you on and keeps you awake.

Years ago, Stephenson gave us his play theory of communication. He sees us using the media in a restorative way. We get home, relax and expand. In front of the TV screen, we have a freedom we don't have in real life vis-à-vis people, police, teachers, the prime minister, sex, violence.

We come with our problems to TV. We come to relax. Believers come to believe. Non-believers come to confirm their non-belief.

When large groups hear parables, people must decide for themselves. Preaching should leave a parable as a parable.

Can we do that too on TV?

Perhaps we can invite people to see and to think. TV cannot be 'interactive'. But perhaps it can provide information that then leads on to communication and meditation. Perhaps we should take another look at the way Jesus talked to the crowds.

We haven't done much when we make a TV programme. TV is not that primary in our communication. Mass media can't change beliefs, only reinforce them. Atheists will be even more convinced. Media can influence opinion only where there are no opinions – or unstable ones.

What about children?

When the home environment is safe, there is no danger in TV. Once personal communication is in order, TV is okay.

One of the few things that communications scholars agree about is that TV can only reinforce. Only personal communication can change people. But if TV replaces the parents as the main introducer to new aspects of reality, the child will face life with a primary reality definition provided by TV.

Would it matter if Christians disappeared from the media?

Very much so. What is not exposed in the media does not seem to exist. At least it is not important. Even though the media may not be the best means of reaching people with the saving gospel of Christ, the presence of a Christian reality definition in the media may be indispensable.

Courage is needed, from those who sit on money, to produce programmes which do what the parables did. These were not very religious. The parables were about true, normal, everyday life. They were about the normal life of a normal citizen.

I propose that we consciously fight the information bias of the mass media by using them in an a communicative way.

*

Don Franco Lever teaches at the Pontifical Salesian University in Rome. In the university, he is the Deputy Director of ISCOS (*Instituto di scienze della comunicazione sociale*.)

Churches think of the media as a tool. They say 'I am the Church. I have the message'.

All the communication nets are changing. There are new tools to understand.

No longer can we just send out the message, all packaged.

We must start with a code. And that is not just a means to transfer an idea. The medium is the means through which I formed the idea. Music is not just a medium to transmit. It's a code to understand myself.

Then how do you use a medium?

When I use film, I can arrive at something which I cannot arrive at in words. A camera is not simply a 'means'. It is a new way of looking at life. To see reality through a viewfinder, helps you think another way.

Too often people inside the Churches think that new media are tools for broadcasting the message to an audience bigger than ever: for them, broadcasting is the novelty; the message remains always the same.

The naivety of this idea is that people are not aware that not only the message but also many other things are changing with the use of the new media. A new medium is not just *transferring* a new message from here to there. It does much more.

How would you explain communication?

Communication is a process with many elements: sender, receiver, context, message, code, voice, channel, codification and decodification. Then, of course, there is feed-back. A new medium organises all these in a new way, and they will work in a different manner.

Let us consider sender, receiver and context. For interpersonal communication – where we use words and non-verbal codes – the receiver has direct control over the context. So he can use some other information (not only what the sender is telling) in order to de-codify the message and to evaluate his truth. On the other side also, the sender has direct control over the context and can intervene to modify the de-codification.

In the case of television, it is not the same. The receiver has no control over the way the sender is organising the message, and the receiver has no control over the situation in which the receiver is watching the programme. They are working in two different contexts. Each is out of the control of the other.

We know that communication today is a very complicated system formed by a lot of different lines crossing each other. Even if some lines are more important than others, they still relate to each other. And then there are crossing points, some more important than others – school, university, clubs, Churches, friends. These are all crossing points with their opinion-leaders and gatekeepers. A new medium re-organises this system of lines. It imposes new structures, a new pace, new leaders.

Writing changed all that – slowly but dramatically. The communication system of the ancient societies, and also the role of many people, had to be transformed.

How has society changed?

Take the role of old people. It is no more necessary to be old in order to be wise or to know the history of the village.

In recent years, television forced the transformation of the radio, of magazines, of newspapers. Also, authority has to act in a different manner than before. Even war is no more the same. In Vietnam, the USA was defeated by its own television and not by the Vietnamese.

A new medium also changes the message. If you pretend to communicate a message with a new medium, don't forget that you are using new signs and new codes. You are assuming new points of view. You are stressing other aspects of the reality. You enter into a new context. Your message – in order to maintain the original meaning – *has to be changed.*

So photography is much more than a craft.

Photography is not just a new way to do some pictures as before. It takes a new kind of pictures. It looks at reality in a different manner. In fact, the painters were obliged to find new ways to make visible their idea of the life and of nature. But the world that photography unveils is not the world of the painters.

Another example can be used. The monk who paints icons is not just translating a written page of theology in the language of colours. With his colours and his brush, he is finding new paths to understand something more of the mystery of God. What he tells in colours can't be told in words.

So what is new in our context is not this or that means of broadcasting a message. In front of us there is a new system of communication, still always changing. Nobody has the recipe of what we have to do. We have to collaborate all together.

The new media help us to understand better the message of God. They are new talents to be used for knowing the tradition, the Bible, our neighbourhood, ourselves, the Lord God is speaking to us through the voices of our contemporaries.

The new media change the system of communication. That means also that communication inside the Church will also change, whether one likes it or not. I don't know but I think that authority is also changing. I don't mean that its importance has to reduce. Its way to act has to find new models.

Communication is a right. It's a right of all men. This is an area where a lot has to be done in order to ensure the rights of many nations and people.

What about the converted?

Of course, the converted need to be reassured and comforted. But, if you trust people that they can understand truth, you can, first of all, prepare the message. Secondly, you can build a situation where they can arrive at the message.

We need a new way to be responsible. We need to be a kind of animator – not just a symbol of authority. Now we have to speak to adults and realise the responsibility of the listener.

Is television a good thing?

I'm not going to pass judgments about positivity or negativity. The air in Rome is sometimes polluted. We have to breathe it. We have to use the media.

Jonah had to go to Nineveh. We have to stay with the media. In the end, Jonah had a change of mind about God. Our task is to go to Nineveh.

How do you teach Communication Studies at ISCOS?

We are at the beginning and so I speak more of my hope than of my experience. We want to take seriously the sciences involved in the studies of human communication: philosophy, semiotics, psychology, sociology, theology. We also study literature, history of art, theatre and the cinema.

We want to prepare people who are able to communicate in our society. That means that we stress training in the different media: the folk media of music and the theatre, print media, electronic media.

Our service is aimed at helping the Church. We want to prepare educators and pastors for the local communities. People who are able to improve communication – with or without the media – and to design new strategies.

We also hope to prepare scholars who will work in order to achieve understanding of what Christian communication is today and what it means for the Church.

*

The Reverend David Holloway is Vicar of Jesmond in England. He is a member of the General Synod of the Church of England. He is an Evangelical and has a wide interest in religious broadcasting.

My communication theory is rooted in incarnational theology. We have to start where people are at.

But so many religious broadcasters think that this means keeping the rumour of God alive, as Robert Foxcroft once said, by simply using *contemporary* concepts or *points of contact*. They

90

assume you have to tell some banal *story* from everyday life, with you sounding daft. Or you have to tell some *recherché* anecdote, with you sounding arrogantly intellectual, and them somehow *sliding* God in. Direct religious talk, they say, is out.

I don't agree. Yes, of course, we sometimes have to do that sort of thing. But generally this approach, with its nervousness of *direct* talk about God-Christ-the Bible fails to take account of how language actually works.

The assumption is that talk about God is completely outside the understanding of many.

People say that we have to try to explain the Christian faith in terms that they can understand. Fine!

But often this fails to take account that after Wittgenstein there has been a new analysis of the way language works and of how we understand concepts and new ideas. Wittgenstein made use of the concept of *games* and others followed him.

How do you explain things? People used to say always by *genus* and *differentia*. 'This is the classification' and 'this is how such and such is different'.

When H.L.A.Hart, the Master of Brasenose College, Oxford, was made Professor of Law he gave an important lecture in which he suggested another way of explaining – if you've got something that's radically different. *Genus* and *differentia* are not the tools to explain things that are unique.

Take something like a trick in a game of cards. How do you explain that? *You explain the game.* You don't say it's 'success in a game' (*genus*) but a 'game of cards' (*differentia*), and then try to compare it with something else to slide the meaning in. You don't say 'It's like a goal in a game of football'. That doesn't help at all. No. You explain it for what it is – something that stands on its own.

My conviction is that Christianity is more this sort of thing. It is unique in the sense that a trick in a game of cards is unique. The substantive part of it stands entirely on its own.

It's no good saying we must get alongside people with *modern* parables. Jesus told parables that 'hearing them, they might not understand'. Parables were for insiders, not outsiders.

Our Christian communication theories are not rigorous enough. That's why American religious broadcasters are quite right when they give a total package. That's the way to understand.

Religious broadcasting in Britain – as anywhere – is, and will be, fundamentally for the religious. But the religious are a huge percentage of the population. Evangelism is a plus. As people overhear religious talk they may begin to understand.

The way religious television will work here is the way Saatchi and Saatchi tried to make television work for the Tory Party at one election time. It was to generate confidence in the committed who would then work better on the streets. It's a background thing to give reinforcement. Most importantly it generates a climate for discourse.

In the United States, the Nielsen Index reveals that the viewing figures for main religious programmes are higher than in the UK. People are seeing religion as a public option.

In Britain and Europe this option is not yet public. We are secular but not secular atheists. We are secular theists. Secularism is where there are no public references to God. They are all *private*. So religion is private. Why does America have more religious activity? Because religion is less private. And TV has a lot to do with that.

Do you fear the future?

Not at all. It's better to have an unpolished Christian programme than a polished one that is sub-Christian. The polish will come in time. The future is going to give us narrowcasting. It will all be a bit more up-market than America, a bit more elegant, but it's going to end up like the American system. We will *indigenise* things a bit. There will be some softening. But there's no doubt about where we are going. Television and radio can put religion on the country's agenda.

Before he became Archbishop of Milan in 1980, Cardinal Carlo Maria Martini was rector of the Pontifical Institute in Rome. He is a Jesuit priest. Succeeding Cardinal Basil Hume, he is the President of the Council of European Bishops' Conferences. He believes that a bishop has to be a President of Communication. In his archdiocese, he has a two-year parish training programme in communication. The first year concentrates on theological and psychological aspects. The second year looks at Family, Diocese and Mass media.

The Church means communication – communication from the Church and within the Church. There is very little free communication within the Church.

The Church communicates in liturgical gestures and gestures of charity. We are too slow, timorous and shy.

Communication is hampered by continuous blockages. They begin in the home – between parents and children. There are too many symptoms of individualism. If they are not dealt with, the media will only increase the sense of alienation.

It is indispensable that we get rid of fears concerning the mass media. They could become real tools in our pastoral work.

Bishops should ask what contact we have with lay communicators.

Do we prepare for the media? Do we spend as much time preparing for a radio interview as we give to preparing for a sermon?

In the past, the Church built hospitals and great cathedrals. Now with one tenth of the money, we could build in the media, not simply to *say something* but so that, through modern icons, there can be a communication of the heart.

CHAPTER 8

But is it broadcasting?

We recommend (to the bishops) that a group be convened, representative of the members and boards of the general Synod, and including persons responsible for Church communication and publicity, to address itself to the following issues:

(a) The development and presentation of an appropriate image of the Church of England for the 1990s... this must include both how the Church understands itself... and how the Church is perceived by others. Greater weight must be given to the work of those responsible for the Church's publicity in matters ranging from the presentation of the General Synod's agenda to the public pronouncements of Church figures...[1]

The Christian Church ought to be the one community on the face of the earth with the ability to differentiate between communication, information and publicity. Almost invariably, these words are used carelessly and interchangeably. Even conversation is confused with the real thing! When we think of communication, we seem to be controlled by an oversized inferiority complex. Instead of going to our communal and scriptural resources, we point instead to the workings of the mass media, failing to realise that they too are themselves already locked on to us in a continual feedback loop. In situations where broadcasting is nationally managed, we Christians are, by majority vote, content to follow the leader. To most of us, a public-service system seems to be the answer. The problem is that many of Europe's Churches received this answer without first knowing the question. History thrust on us a European version of the 'sweetheart deal'. But if there had been a choice or a crossroads, is public-service broadcasting the avenue we should have chosen? Now after three score years and ten, the *status quo* has been upset. A new set of answers is on the way. Whether or not the Churches have any control over their own broadcasting destiny will depend entirely on our own curiosity about communication and our self-confidence in our own special insights.

Hardly surprisingly, the Christian Churches are producing too few media idealists or creative artists. And the ones we have are undervalued and underfunded. Of course, we can each make our personal list of exceptions. In most of these, the IKON Christian production house in the Netherlands would appear near the top. But for the most part Christians are not renowned for their current creativity. Perhaps in such a market-driven enterprise, we have every excuse. Could Robert Bresson's *Au hasard, Balthazar*, a Christian parable through the eyes of a donkey, be made today? *Jesus of Montreal* has been made but how many Church synods would have put up the seed money, and for what pay-off? In any case, in such an over-commercialised broadcasting system creativity is diminished. Religious patrons of the television arts have less influence. Control has passed into the hands of an all-powerful new gatekeeper. The search is on, not for authenticity but for any bright idea that the producer will buy. So Christian broadcasting in Europe is too boringly centrist. There are no Left or Right wings, no revolutionaries.

Communities are provoked and led forward by their extremists. Christianity is no exception and subsists in the words and actions of an *avant garde* founder. But there are not too many television radicals. If there are dreamers, they do not seem to be waking. Once, there were monasteries where monks spent years on their illuminated scrolls. Why are they not painting new icons in electronic colours? We have turned an art form into a market place. Significantly, the Montreal Jesus did not go into the temple and overthrow the tables of the money-changers. He went instead into a TV studio and threw down the cameras and lights. Broadcasting idealists do exist in Europe. Some are Christian. Many are not. But they all deserve to have their portrait in an album such as this.

However, more than any other group of people, they will realise that too many snapshots can soon induce fatigue and inattention. When this happens, the proud photographer is simply reduced to meditating. Message-sending comes to an untimely end.

*

"Do you want another hour with the BBC or would you rather meet a radical video-maker?"

The question came with Ulster directness. An answer was hardly required. In fact, they were a quartet of video artists and occupied some seedy rooms next to a libertarian bookshop, not far from Belfast's much-televised Lower Falls Road. Belfast Independent Video is a co-operative. By special dispensation of Britain's ACTT union, they are a registered franchised workshop and they have made a number of programmes for Britain's Channel 4. *Moving Myths* is a religious production about the 'survivors' of Irish religion. It looks critically at people who were brought up within the Protestant and Catholic churches but who now regard themselves as atheists. A radical theme? Perhaps. But the real radicalism is contained in the media outlook of at least some of the producers. They claim that people are not simply subjects to be filmed. The recorded image is not the absolute property of the film-maker, to be cut, mixed and altered at will. The actors too must have a voice in the production. They can be involved in the planning for the way in which they will set out their personality and their cause. So the finished product does not rely solely on the creative genius of the director. Everyone is involved.

Every conceivable objection can be used against such a production technique. Most of them would begin with the immortal words: "In the real world..." The idea is costly, time-consuming and impractical. "In the end, someone has to make a decision." "You couldn't do that in Tienanmen Square!". "This kind of thing would de-skill the director!" "It sounds more like social work than film-making!" On the other hand, there are some who hope that principle and practice can sometimes co-exist. There is a larger number who, while they do not chain themselves to railings, are glad that others sometimes have done so. They may not themselves

96

be organic eaters. They may not be personally over-fussed about what or whom they eat. But because some people erect an extreme marker, others are sensitised. If this were not so, it would be rather difficult to justify St. Francis of Assisi and other survivors of religion.

*

"Can local television be significant?"

"I think it is rather unimportant at this stage." Stig Svärd directs a government agency that subsidises the arts. He also happens to be a Baptist minister. In Stockholm, he is best known for his close political links and for his encyclopaedic knowledge of broadcasting legislation.

"At this stage" he is right. Wherever in the world there is a cable station, there is the capability to feed in community programming to take its place alongside the commercial networks. But the theory is not often put into practice. Local access is a media dream, waiting to be realised. In the United States, because they are under-resourced, significant community access channels are few and far between. Local material is handled much more successfully by local commercial stations. In Sweden there are special circumstances. The country's democracy cannot be understood outside the context of the major social building blocks (the *folkrörelser*) – the labour unions, the teetotallers, the Social Democratic party and the folk Church. At one level, this gives community access a head start compared with the situation and political philosophy in many other parts of Europe. The disadvantage is that, up till 1990, advertising and concealed sponsorship has been forbidden. And the ban has been strictly enforced. Everything depends on the declining fortunes and convoluted discussions of the Social Democrats. Without advertising revenue, the future of the country's 18 local cable television services will remain difficult.

Malmö is in the extreme South West of the country. Denmark is so close that Copenhagen is the favoured airport. A very wide range of international television is available. Ninety thousand householders, four-fifths of the city's population, are on cable and are, therefore, potential viewers for 'Malmö's own TV station'. Anders Lageson is jointly employed by the Lutheran parishes of the area. Each year

97

he produces thirty-two editions of his magazine programme *Meeting Place* (*Möteplats*), as well as a significant number of specials. For Anders Lageson, local television is not in any way a poor cousin of national broadcasting. In many ways it is a superior medium, particularly for religious broadcasting. Indeed, it is national coverage that is, so often, a short cut. "I have one great advantage," says Anders Lageson. "I can show something to my viewers who can then do their own reality check. My programmes ring true with familiar sights, buildings and faces. The viewer can go round to this or that church. He can know for himself that everything is real – the instructors in the local swimming pool, the library, a school orchestra in a town-centre church."

In 1988, Malmö had its own Advent calendar programme. It was a Herculean but inexpensive production. Twenty-nine 15–minute programmes and, needless to say, the city's schoolchildren each had their own calendar and learned a special song. Technical quality is high but there seems to be no need for state-of-the-art equipment. Anders Lageson works with low-band Umatic equipment and is happy to improvise. When the Christian pop star Laila Dahl visited the town, he sent one cameraman to film her in a local park. She spoke of her faith and was, of course, asked to sing her hit 'After the Rain'. Synchronisation was provided by the simplest of cassette players. When she came to the line "and the sun broke through", the totally unrehearsed cameraman simply pointed his lens at the sky. The sun, obligingly, broke through.

One of the most commonly-expressed objections to the whole idea of Christian broadcasting is that it depicts a Church that does not exist. An earnest, well-prepared preacher exhorting a large, well-illuminated, generation-spanning, smiling and ecumenical congregation may in fact be a thoroughly detached spectacle – an enticing but personally-unconvincing fiction. Some people enjoy watching. But then they also used to enjoy watching heroic cowboys (who never existed) shooting native American (who certainly did). But, simply watching does not make viewers want to go anywhere near a cowboy. Still less does it make them wish they had been born native Americans. So Christian broadcasting is tied in its own knot. The more attractive the Church of the airwaves becomes, the more detached it becomes from the building down the road or the old man next door who attends. As far as Anders Lageson is concerned, the scale on which he operates answers the criticism. "We are different," he says. "The difference is that our TV actually reinforces reality. Perhaps it's the adults who need it most. In children's TV, the familiar things are more universal. They can identify with nursery equipment and pools. For children these things are universal."

*

Local, in European broadcasting, can mean almost anything. Local radio, in particular, can cover a large part of Scotland or a tiny part of an Italian parish. The new opportunities in broadcasting mean differences of focus and of scale. Macro or micro, the world's Christians contrive to be idealists in ways that are wonderful and various. At one end of the scale are those who praise God for the satellites and a means to blanket half the globe with gospel television. On the other side, there is a quieter company who sees tiny community radio as a means of restoring health to the malformed urban sprawl, or as a way of giving confidence to under-represented minorities. Disappointingly, the European Christians in this second group are vastly outnumbered.

In the Third World, and particularly in South America, community-sized radio is a development and educational tool, something to facilitate two-way contact. The pioneer in this field was the Christian educator Paulo Freire and the Roman Catholic Church remains heavily involved. Protestant broadcasting can be large-scale. The Voice of the Andes from Quito blankets the continent. However, it is easy to make sweeping generalisations. The Catholic *Radio Veritas*, which broadcasts from Manila, is hardly a village radio. It played its part in toppling a government. So is it possible to make a simple distinction between community broadcasting and an alternative, market-driven form of local broadcasting? "We are talking about a type of broadcasting that responds to community concerns because it belongs to and is part of the community," says AMARC which is the French acronym for the World Association of Community Broadcasters. "This type of participatory communication does a lot more than sell soap. It is an agent for cultural development, democratisation and social change."

But European community radio has developed in two separate ways. There are stations that express locality – a voluntary public service to the civil parish. At this level many local churches are involved. Alternatively, there has been a strong European tendency for community radio to reflect interest groups, movements and special causes within the community. Afficionados could just as easily be involved in computer networking or the alternative press. In several countries (Ireland is but one example), community broadcasters are recently-reformed radio pirates. Of course there are also commercial stations that target the ethnic communities. Is it just the advertising support that keeps London's Sunrise Radio and Spectrum Radio out of the AMARC camp? Unusually in Europe, Britain's new breed of community radios must, in the words of British government minister David Mellor, raise all their funds "out of their own resources and those of their own supporters". At its most worthwhile, community radio represents minorities taking their own initiative in affirming their own identity. *Radio Judaica* is the fifth free radio in Brussels and, at the same time, Europe's leading Jewish radio. Europe's Jews have good cause not to be too idealistic. M. Rahmani, one of *Radio Judaica's* patrons, is a pragmatist: "I think that what is useful in this world of radio is that our culture has been discovered. For example, there are some people who are stupefied to discover that we speak French."[2]

Some broadcasting idealists think in hemispheric terms. For others the village boundary is quite far enough. 'Pie in the sky' or 'parish pump', in the 1990s the electronic media have something for everyone. But just because so much is available (all of it loosely grouped under the misnomer of 'broadcasting'), is everything equally acceptable? Is a community radio with two hundred listeners just as worthwhile as a great scheme to evangelise the earth? More to the point, should Christians actively discriminate between broadcasting options? Is Anders Lageson right? Could small mean more beauty, and less danger?

Piet Derksen is an altogether different kind of broadcasting idealist. A Dutch multi-millionaire, he is identified with Christian broadcasting on the grandest scale. A Roman Catholic, he underwent as an adult a profound religious conversion experience. He is known as a Charismatic Catholic and this is true. But other adjectives are needed for he is a man of contradictions. He is theologically conservative, or at least traditional. On the other hand there is an impulsive streak that sometimes makes him innocently receptive to a new idea. His primary interest is world evangelisation and, on that level only, he is ecumenical. With this world's goods, he is very well-endowed. He once owned the Dutch sports goods retailing chain *Sporthuis Centrum*. He is a controversial figure even in Catholic circles. Rumour suggests a church within a church, a mixture of *Opus Dei* and Freemasonry, a religious Goldfinger (more Catholic than the Pope) with a godly plot to stop the world with Christian Television from space. Protestants divide along an easily predicted fault-line. To liberals, Derksen is a shadowy capitalist, the backer of yet another version of right wing televangelism. To Evangelicals and Charismatics he is, on the whole, good news – apart, of course, from his Romishness.

The truth may be more straightforward. Now an old man, Piet Derksen's spiritual spring has been the Catholic Charismatic movement. He has been deeply influenced by the French *Emmanuel* community which has a central devotion to the Sacred Heart of Jesus. He makes no bones about his belief in television as a tool for evangelisation. His staff, at least, claim to be fully aware of the danger of transmitting trans-cultural material. A weekly television magazine programme, *Lumen 2,000*, is produced in Dallas. It has audiences in North and South America but so far does not appear in Europe. Derksen's staff speak of their strict policy against buying airtime. In Dallas there is a media training school and a major video bank which might be interested in working with Protestants "but only if the purpose of the exercise is evangelisation". *Lumen 2,000* (the name has also long been used of the worldwide Derksen movement) works on the ground as well as from space in a number of countries. There are strong *Lumen 2,000* organisations in South America and help has been given to consolidate new religious programmes on Polish public television. "We are not even a corporation," says Piet Derksen. "We are more of a movement for evangelisation." The movement's worldwide clearing-house is in Eindhoven.

Piet Derksen's definition of Christian broadcasting has the virtue of great clarity. He also is a broadcasting idealist. Nowadays there are many like him in Europe, both Roman Catholic and Protestant. Some have long complained of media persecution. Now they are being offered new opportunities – or at least a wider range of narrower opportunities in which to give expression to their idealism. Of course many North European Churches continue to place their trust in public-service broadcasting. It has many advantages, not least that it costs the Church nothing and, however small the cake, the mainstream is guaranteed its generous slice. But this is to be cynical. Public service is also an ideal. It has, and deserves to have, true believers. It does one thing outstandingly well which the new Europe will forget at its peril. Public-service broadcasting cannot by definition be monopolised by those with something urgent and particular to say.

So whether broadcasting is large-scale or small-scale, there are two quite different Christian ideals. This has been particularly clearly revealed in the debate, both inside and outside Parliament, about Britain's new Broadcasting legislation. "We have come within a hair's breadth of having all religious broadcasting banned," said one prominent campaigner, Gareth Littler of the Council for Christian Standards in Society. No doubt he meant what he said but clearly he was not counting all those public-service programmes that could be said to be seen through the eye of a sensitive fly-on-the-wall – not an evangelistic creature but an observer of other people's religious experience. Probably, in the Derksen sense, these are not Christian programmes. So the idealists are clearly divided. "We are talking of cool media," said Ernest Rea of the BBC. "What the campaigners want is a different model. Ethnic group would talk to ethnic group with each community sitting under its own figtree."

*

A final souvenir (a 'snapshot' taken by many people) not of a broadcasting idealist but of the idealised broadcaster. It stands in London, in the entrance hall of Broadcasting House. It is a statue of The Sower and it is by Eric Gill, whose place in the history of art was secured, ironically, not so much by his sculpture but by his contributions to typography – which Broadcasting House has done its own little bit to supplant. The sculpture is a simple anonymous figure. In the way that walruses and seals all seem to look alike, it lacks a personality. This is not Zebedee-the-Sower. This is The Sower and there is nothing to know about him apart from his task in life. So Gill's statue is fluid, faceless and full of movement. The

102

arm is across the body, taking another palmful for yet another broadcast of seed. This of course is the familiar idealisation of broadcasting. The Sower scatters his seeds in a great arc. Some will fall on stony ground but some will find fertile soil, bear fruit and multiply. But the imagery is not altogether helpful. It may help explain how the gospel works. It certainly does nothing to explain the electronic mass media.

Nowadays, even farming has changed. Seeds are not scattered by broadcast. Every seed is targeted to its predetermined place and depth. Planting takes place according to a precise pattern. Soil humidity, the depth of each drill, even the weather – all is known in advance. But to return just once more to The Sower's dead art, nowadays, audiences are targeted – not with an old shotgun but with a sniper's rifle. This means that, in market-driven broadcasting, audiences are identified and maximised and their preferences are noted. So there is no more 'seed'. The audience is entertained. And it is possible to make a philosophical justification for getting what you want. "Right now you get what other people think is good for you," says Teresa Gorman, the British MP. In the 1930s, at the beginning of The Sower's brief return to life, his broadcasting gave what he thought was good. It took place, as far as his technology would allow, over the length and breadth of his native lands. The political boundaries of the nation state were seen as his only field-markers. But everything has changed. Broadcasting is not only becoming international and homogeneous. At the very same time, it is becoming much more local. It is also 'narrowing'. Christians, quite rightly, have not forgotten The Sower, but if they look for him in modern farms or in the corridors of broadcasting companies, they will look in vain. Broadcasters forgot about The Sower long ago.

References

[1] From *Call to Order: Vocation and Ministry in the Church of England.* ACCM.

[2] Reported in French by Sybille d'Oiron in *Features. Un Magazin pour l'Europe* of the Robert Schuman Institute, Brussels.

CHAPTER 9

Home Services in close-up

When men of Eric Gill's profession speak of a 'detail', the word is used in a special way. In the graphic arts, a detail is a small portion, separated from the whole and viewed on its own. This chapter contains two such details. They depict the religious broadcasting of two North European neighbours. Similar examinations could have been made in almost any part of Europe. Nowadays Albania is the only exception and even this may be temporary. In Britain, commercial broadcasting is entering a newly deregulated period. David Mellor, the Home Office minister with responsibilty for placing the new Broadcasting Bill before Parliament, had drawn the sting of most his critics by an unusual openness to last-minute suggestions, criticisms and ideas. "We're not consulting the Lord God Almighty on these issues," he once remarked on a British television programme. In the event, he consulted nearly everyone else.

In the run-up to the new British broadcasting Act, there had been an undeclared civil war between Evangelicals and the mainstream. "The problem is the unholy alliance between the Home Office and the Church hierarchy," complained one Whitehall Trojan Horse. On the other hand, mainstream churchmen suspected that Downing Street might buckle under a powerful hose of petitions and delegations for freedom to preach the gospel. This of course would undermine the cosy (if not exactly holy) alliance between the Churches and Britain's broadcasting duopoly. If religious broadcasting could be undertaken by private entrepreneurs, what arguments could be employed for its continued maintainance out of the public purse? In the end both religious groups were left hoarse and with an uneasy suspicion that each had emerged a loser. A much more significant watershed for public-service broadcasting will be the renewal of the BBC Royal Charter in 1996.

If we had decided to take as our detail the situation in the South of Europe, in Iberia or Italy, a great number of wholly-owned religious broadcasting operations would be revealed. After half a century of Catholic radio, *Rádio Renascença* has been all but promised one of Portugal's two new television channels. In Germany, on the other hand, the established churches continue to occupy an acknowledged and seemingly secure position in the broadcasting services of each of the *Länder*. But in France, since 1986, religious broadcasters are having to pay their own way. In the Netherlands the religious output continues to depend upon the number of members of each of the various broadcasting associations.

In the East, Christian communicators are still coping with the after-shock; getting rid of a subtle enemy, whom Poland's new broadcasting chief, Dr. Andrzej Drawicz, calls "the Devil of reversed ideas". Meanwhile, in the North, the future health of Swedish public-service broadcasting continues to depend on crucial political decisions on advertising by the much-weakened Social Democrats. Denmark and Norway are not large countries and both have to rely heavily on imported programmes. English is a second language and, partly because their culture could so easily be overwhelmed, a public-service broadcasting philosophy is still strongly promoted by politicians, trade unions and community organisations. The folk Churches of both countries certainly do not exercise overt influence over national radio and television. However they continue to be well-represented. At the same time alternative channels are increasingly available.

In the beginning, this book set out to be an album of photographs of Europe's enormous media landscape. This chapter will contain just two enlargements and provide a closer, detailed look at the religious broadcasting of Denmark and then Norway. But personally-selected snapshots, especially close-ups, can be too much for some readers. Those who prefer a broader perspective may hope to find one outside Europe, on the Sea of Galilee, in Chapter 10.

Alternatively, from a final aerial viewpoint, some tentative suggestions are put forward in Chapter 11.

AUNT BETTY IN JUTLAND

The vast majority of the Danish population belongs to the state Lutheran Church. In the 1960s, the Church seemed to be losing ground. The number of church weddings, baptisms and confirmations declined. Now some of that ground has been regained and confirmation remains a significant milestone in most young people's lives. Perhaps it is more of a family occasion than a strictly religious sacrament. But its popularity does at least place the Church within the life of most families. The state Church has a great commitment to social work and public health care in which its deaconesses are strongly active. However, Danish Lutheranism is in one sense 'headless'. There is no archbishop and no synod. The Church is said to be priest-orientated. Each priest is in large measure autonomous. The strongest centripetal force is exerted by the government's ministry for Church affairs. Recent attempts to discipline a small number of clergy who have been open to New Age ideas or who expressed interest in the notion of reincarnation, have pointed up the Church's lack of organisational authority.

In the last century, the greatest single influence on the mainstream of the Danish Church was N.F.S.Grundtvig. A hymn writer, theologian, Danish cultural historian and preacher, Grundtvig re-defined the major role of the Danish Church. He believed that the oral word is the living word and that this word is not read but told. Today, the Church's Lutheran theological label is no guarantee against internal division. The *Indre Mission* (Home Mission) is conservative, some would say cautious, and – like everything else – autonomous. The *Tidehverv* (turning of the tide) movement, on the other hand, is extremely Lutheran and would see the gospel as the forgiveness of sins and nothing else. Its attitude to broadcasting would be that the word of God is the word of God and simply needs to be proclaimed. A church full of empty pews is but a sign that the gospel has been rejected.

On February 25th, 1925 the first religious service was broadcast on the new state radio. The following year a Christian Listening Organisation was formed and, on the grounds that it could muster

21,000 members, it was allowed two representatives on the Radio Council. In 1928 the first full-time religious consultant was appointed to Danish Radio. Among other tasks, he had to approve the broadcasting of non-Lutheran services. A pattern for the broadcasting of religious worship was evolved and this remained intact until the beginning of the 1980s. Services were broadcast at 10 am and 5 pm on Sundays. In the summer, the 5 pm service was transposed to 8 in the morning. From 1926 until today, short morning services have been broadcast on Radio One from Copenhagen Cathedral.

In 1970 a religious producer Jörgen Thorgard developed studio based services instead of the second Sunday service and, from 1975, a morning reflection *Ved Dagens Begyndelse* (At the beginning of the day) was broadcast at 6.55 am and 8.55 am on Radio One. This was the brainchild of the new head of religious radio, Mogens Hansen. It provided the only place in Denmark where laymen could preach. Using an informal 'Coffee Club', Hansen and his colleagues selected the group who filled the *Beginning of the day* slot for one week at a time. Many of these five-day series were later published as books and booklets.

In the 1970s, Mogens Hansen abandoned the hope that all clergy could broadcast effectively. He tried to educate twelve priests in the ways of radio. Members of *Tidehverv* opposed the idea of human selection. This was a time of experiment and services were shortened for broadcasting. The Sunday morning programme on Radio One is still presented by Mogens Hansen with Anders Laugesen. It is listened to by an audience equal in number to Denmark's Sunday churchgoers. Danish religious broadcasting is changing in various and subtle ways. Despite its considerable weight in society, the Danish Church has no special access. The broadcasting monopoly was charged to be impartial. However, no-one can deny that the national Church has been given very fair treatment.

Danish broadcasting became the monopoly of *Danmarks Radio* in the 1920s. But in the last few years there has been a quiet revolution. Since 1989 there has been an alternative television service, TV2, which buys its programmes from outside producers. It was hoped that this breaking of the monopoly would result in many more religious programmes. Independent local radio and television is also permitted and, as laws prohibiting advertising have been relaxed, operates on an increasingly commercial basis. It is relatively easy to start a local radio station. For example the Copenhagen district of Frederiksberg works through a three-man commission. When franchises are issued, applications are sifted, channels are allocated and smaller groups are called together and asked to share the available time 'blocks'. Eighty per cent of the population are said to listen to local radio at some time. There is a local radio fund to which the poorer organisations can apply on the basis of their transmission hours. Some of the larger stations have found ways of over-exploiting this source and, rather than trying to close all the loopholes, there is now talk of abolishing the fund altogether.

Local radio began in Denmark in 1985. Regulation is light. There are no requirements about technical standards. Stations are connected to the transmitters by telephone line. Religious groups are permitted to be sole owners of local radios. However, all transmissions must be logged and recordings must be retained for three months. There are, however, strict rules against networking. By far the largest local station is Copenhagen's The Voice. Running costs always include performing rights charges to *Gramex* and *Coda*, the telephone and transmission standing charges and a levy for the local radio fund. Even Copenhagen's tiny Roman Catholic community has its own local station in *Radio Steno*. It broadcasts from a school-based studio for three hours on Sundays. Like a relay runner handing over the baton, *Radio Steno* (named after the Catholic Dane who discovered the lymphatic system) then hands over to one of the other three stations who share the frequency.

When local broadcasting began, there were ninety stations of which twenty-five had a religious orientation. Of those, thirteen were Free Church (Pentecostal and others), five were conservative Lutheran (*Indre Mission*) and seven were ecumenical. There are now three religious local TV stations. The biggest and the first is KKR which is owned by two Copenhagen churches (Elim Pentecostal Church and Taka Church). The Executive Group, consisting of elders from the two churches, bought a disused dairy. The building cost nearly D.Kr.2 million. To try to make ends meet, KKR now produces some secular material. KKR is the only survivor of the idealistic (not necesarily religious) groupings who, six years earlier, entered the brave new world of local television testing. KKR specialises in follow-up ministry. It has an interdenominational representative committee which includes members of all the Danish Churches. It practises a very open policy towards other Churches and helped to produce – and then screened – a programme on *Catholics in Denmark*.

Birger Lind, KKR's Director, believes he has proved the point that "you can do Christian television". Broadcasts now go out on two frequencies for a total of thirty-four hours a week and two company names are required: KKR and Channel 7. The companies are now permitted to make in-house advertisements for customers. KKR/Channel 7 covers 802,000 potential households. In addition, two other Christian stations in Aalborg (*TV-Inter*) and Aarhus (*TV-Inter*) cover 175,000 households and 249,000 households respectively. Theoretically programme coverage includes three-quarters of the Danish population but KKR's financial position is critical. The station and its eighteen paid staff face immense financial problems. Each year, D.Kr.7 million is required and KKR is raising only half of that amount. A 1990 televised appeal for help raised D.Kr.750,000 from 900 callers. Prudently, the KKR managers are reluctant to repeat this exercise too often. KKR runs on a two-month reserve and the strain is telling. The company's best hope is that other denominations, and especially Denmark's large Lutheran Church, will buy time segments. One agency of the national Church, the highly conservative *Indre Mission*, has agreed to take a half-hour weekly slot for D.Kr.500,000.

Like many Evangelical broadcasters in Europe, KKR takes an overly pessimistic line on public-service religious programmes: "The latest news is that the national TV has cut off the remnants they had of Christian programmes and the new TV2 still has nearly no Christian programmes!" On the other hand, when KKR re-uses material from the United States (Pat Robertson's *700 Club* is one example), the more intense healings and prophesyings are deleted. The film *Halifax 672 did not return*, a KKR co-production with the Canadian TV preacher David Mainse, is an original and professional treatment of the shooting-down over Denmark of a man who later became a Roman Catholic priest.

Another significant Christian programme producer is the Christian Media Centre in Viborg (*Danmarks Kirkelige Mediecenter*). It is a business *fond* owned by no less than forty-five organisations and its stated purpose is to make programmes. There are only two full-time staff but in 1989, buying in production staff from the market place, the Centre made seven programmes for the new TV2 channel. The director, Benny Aros, an ex-journalist, foresees an increasing output. Among the first programmes was one on the papal visit to Denmark. Other productions included a Christian series for children and, a typically Danish theme, fairy tales for Christmas. The Centre makes videos for its member organisations and also some radio programmes. There are also media-training courses and productions for local TV including Denmark's well-known *TV Lorry*. From its impressive first year's output, the Centre earned about twenty-five per cent of its income. The remainder comes from a reserve fund of D.Kr.10 million which, over the next two or three years, will be doubled. Most of this money will have come from two anonymous donors. The Centre is not allowed to use more than ten per cent of its reserve in any one year. Support comes from across the Danish church spectrum. Benny Aros believes that his production house could not function without the buying power of TV2 and most important of all, his growing financial cushion. However the Centre is still held back for lack of money. Aros would like to move into animation.

So much for Denmark's new religious broadcasting. In a sense these are still fringe activities. One of them, the Viborg Centre, seems full of optimism. Another, KKR, retains its idealism but is having to face the possibility of closure. The present still belongs to the state broadcasting system, to *Danmarks Radio* - a monopoly no longer - and its evolving relationship with Denmark's Churches. From the beginning, the first Church consultant, Gunnar Engberg, declared that he wished to be "as honest as I can be as an independent Church consultant." To this day, irate letters from bishops on programming and scheduling policy have very little effect. Mogens Hansen puts the same independent point of view but with greater sharpness: "Danish Radio has no greater obligation towards the folk church, or the other Churches or organisations, than we have towards the Danish railway or the State postal service".

There is a new, if long-term, risk to the position of religious broadcasting in the schedules of Danish radio and television. A reorganisation has done away with old specialisms in favour of a new breed of directors each in charge of morning, afternoon, and weekend schedules. The immediate result for programme quality has been good. However, the religious segment more than ever stands or falls on its own inherent quality and audience figures. Unlike some of the other Nordic countries, there is no overall head of religious television or radio.

Hansen sees the purpose of religious broadcasting as: "Reaching the sick and housebound, fulfilling a popular need for devotion and hymn singing and giving 'strangers' a taste of religion." Most Danish religious broadcasters have been prepared to experiment and adapt but a conservative alternative view persists to the present day. Jörgen Bögh, Dean of Aarhus, and sometime anti-market MEP, believed that there should be no special presentation of the gospel. The media must adapt to sermons and not the other way round. Jan Arvid Hellestrom, a Swede, and perhaps the leading media thinker in the Nordic countries, summarises the two opposing views. "The major tension in religious broadcasting is the problem of being a mere mirror which reflects the services and the parishes... and the principle of putting religious broadcasting into a more media-friendly form."

Until the 1970s, Danish religious broadcasting was simply a mirror. "Radio", according to producer Anders Laugesen, "was simply the big loudspeaker." Like most of the staff of *Danmarks Radio*, Anders Laugesen occupies a centralist broadcasting position. He wants to stimulate and interest those on the edge of the national folk Church but is aware of the criticisms of some Evangelicals who see this as a sell-out, a misused opportunity to preach the gospel. An important development has been the idea of the radio workshop. Issues are worked at in a three-part sequence. Feedback from listeners decides on the direction of the following programme. Radio workshops have covered ethical issues, and even a phrase-by-phrase discussion of parts of Denmark's new Bible translation.

Laugesen is the co-producer of Radio One's Sunday programme which has 200,000 listeners. He has questionings of his own. He wants to talk the language of 'Aunt Betty in Jutland' but he wonders if he is pandering to Aunt Betty's seeming inability to attend a real Sunday service. On the other hand, perhaps Danish religious broadcasting (the public-service variety) does in fact match some national characteristics: a great emphasis on the spoken word, an often-brilliant use of the fairy tale motif and the love of discussion. Perhaps public service broadcasting also reinforces a widespread tradition of rather nominal Church membership or, put another way, it dovetails neatly with a Church which, in its worship, encourages, in Anders Laugesen's words, a "rather anonymous feeling".

NORWAY'S 'LARGEST CHURCH'

Ask Norwegians to say what is distinctive about their country's Lutheran church and they will probably answer "Pietism". In Norwegian terms, this means something like "Conservative Evangelical" but with a shading of Wesleyan holiness, and perhaps a diminished emphasis on door knocking. Much of its strength comes from a Norwegian adverse reaction to German liberal theology.

The Norwegian state Church is episcopal but is visibly content that its bishops (like the Danish bishops) stand outside the apostolic succession. Like Finland (but unlike Sweden) those Norwegians who were influenced by pietism remained within the Church. The result is that in many parishes in the West and South, prayer houses grew up. Those who attended each prayer house (*bedehus*) still belonged to the national Church. They could remain occasional, or frequent, communicants at the parish Church. However, each conventicle, and there might be several in a parish, had a life of its own.

The *Bedehus* movement has deeply affected the Norwegian church. In alliance with biblically-conservative clergy, the movement gave birth to the Free Faculty of Theology in Oslo where eight of Norway's ten present bishops were trained. A still more important result was the growth of the missions – two home missions, based in Oslo and Bergen, and three foreign missions that give Norway more missionaries per head of population than any country after New Zealand. The folk Church still occupies an important place within Norwegian society. Ninety per cent of the population are formal members of the Church of Norway. Five per cent of all Norwegians are active members of the national Church while a similar percentage are churchgoing members of one of the free denominations. To the pollsters' question "Are you a personal Christian?" up to twenty per cent of the entire population regularly answer "Yes".

NRK, the Norwegian broadcasting corporation, has been described as the country's largest church. This is reflected in some of the audience statistics. Nearly twenty per cent of Norwegians claim to listen to traditional devotions on national radio. Fifteen per cent tune to televised worship on Sundays. On Thursday evenings the audience for the religious programmes on national television (there is only one channel) is an outstanding twenty-five per cent. Even NRK's religious producers regard this figure with a happy suspicion. The Thursday programme is well-placed and comes immediately before the main evening news. It is not simply a religious discussion programme. Its purpose includes preaching.

In both broadcasting and religious terms Norway may be a European special case. For ten years, the country has been talking about a second TV channel, probably financed by advertisements. Decisions have not yet been made. For a decade, local radio, local television and cable television have been permitted. European and Scandinavian satellites are offering their wares both to the cable companies and to the growing number of dish owners. From the beginning, and despite its firm place in national life, the Norwegian national Church has never *owned* religious broadcasting on NRK. Indeed there has never been a radio committee on the British model. Sometimes the Church has staffed special advisory groups but only on a single-project basis. There have been occasional demands from the religious pressure group KKL for more devotional services, but these have been resisted, particularly by the national television service. NRK TV is allowed to buy in. Occasionally, the Religious Department does authorise programmes that have been independently-produced. They have to speak "our film language".

NRK is now having to face some tight budgeting. Its only source of income is from TV licence fees. Much of NRK's available money is now spent supporting a policy of decentralisation which will help it to face the competition from the long-awaited TV2 channel. About forty-five per cent of NRK's programmes are of foreign origin. Many are from the BBC. NRK is still completely committed to the public service ideal. Producers feel that religious broadcasting will continue to be safe because Norwegian broadcasting was born into an environment heavily influenced by the Church and the country's labour movement. Interestingly, religious broadcasting is exempt from the general direction to NRK not to be propagandist. Religion has a particular strong presence on P1, one of the two national radio services. For the last six years, a representative Christian group has managed morning *Andakt* items, broadcast on four mornings a week.

NRK's broadcasting monopoly came to an end on May 1st, 1988. Local radio and local television stations could be licensed and, in principle, the licence applied to one locality only. Several high ideals were expressed: freedom of speech for minorities, the strengthening of local identities and dialects, local ownership, local productions. Franchises last for five years for radio and seven years for television. Advertisements are allowed for up to six minutes per hour. No advertisements are allowed on major Christian holidays. There is a sixteen per cent gross tax which, as in Denmark, supports poorer relations in local broadcasting. Other sources of income include subsidies from some municipalities and bingo.

Norway has an amazing 465 local radios for its four million people. Some are big and successful with ten to fourteen employees. Many have no full-time staff. Out of the total population in 1989, seventy-four per cent could listen to local radio and twenty per cent did. Local radios broadcast for 350,000 hours a year. (The government puts the figure at 500,000 but the local radio association, the *Norsk Naerradioforbud*, refuses to count 'automated all-night music machines'.) Ten thousand volunteers and 1,500 paid employees are involved. All *naerradio* is FM. In Oslo, fifty local radio stations have to share six frequencies. There are ninety Christian radios and thirty to forty 'umbrella' stations in which local Churches play some part. In a further ten secular radios, there is some Christian input. The Pentecostals are skilled and experienced in local radio and as far as the state church is concerned, one of the missions – the *Misjonssambandet* - is particularly active. It has a media school in Kristiansand and a background of short-wave broadcasting from Monte Carlo and from Guam.

In local broadcasting, advertising is allowed on radio but not in local television. This means that the latter operates on idealism and philanthropy and the financial situation is often parlous. Ironically, in view of the tight leash on local television, there are no laws about satellite broadcasting on the Norwegian statute book. There are two satellite services TV3 and TVN on which there is occasional religious broadcasting. In 1990, there was a curious role reversal. NRK broadcast Norway's premier ski contest while a satellite company transmitted·the skiers' special Sunday service!

Hans Bratterud trained at Oral Roberts University in Tulsa, Oklahoma. He was President of European Religious Broadcasters and is probably Norway's premier exponent of evangelisation by satellite. So far, however, his effect has been slight and he is distanced from Norway's active Pentecostal congregations. Oslo's *Filadelfia* Pentecostal church is almost a megachurch of North American proportions. It leads a group consisting of Methodists, Baptists and the ubiquitous *Indre Mission* in taking time on one of Oslo's stations. Twelve of the thirty Christian hours are filled by *Filadelfia's* own *Sentrum Radio*.

The aim is straightforward – winning new members and follow-up. This appears to be succesful. With help from the Swedish Pentecostal group, TV Inter, the *Filadelfia* congregation is planning a major investment in evangelistic television. They are wary of the money-raising approach of Hans Bratterud. Apart from building up a subscribers' association, they are relying on the business acumen and generosity of their own congregation. At present they appear only occasionally on TV Oslo which can reach up to 900,000 people. The evidence suggests that, when a local church has a programme of evangelistic mission and also uses local radio in a kind of pincer movement, there can be a marked increase in membership. *Filadelfia's* first televised Bible Marathon raised N.Kr.420,000 for Russian bibles. The Church claimed 1,200 converts in four days. Four weeks later, seventy per cent of those attending its weekly 'Open House' were said to be ('invited-by-television') strangers. In one year, a free Lutheran Church in Frederikstad committed no less than half its budget to radio outreach.

The budget of the Norwegian state Church is funded from taxes collected by the government. In 1989 each Norwegian taxpayer paid N.Kr.320, the price of a pair of shoes, for the Church. But money is still the Church's problem and one of the saddest stories, from the point of view of communication, is the tale of IMMI. It was founded in 1977 by Sig Aske, General Secretary of Norwegian Church Aid, closely associated with Radio Voice of the Gospel and a former Director of Media for the Lutheran World Federation. His vision was for Christian involvement in mass communications and, in particular, for religious broadcasting by satellite.

In 1985 IMMI in turn founded Eikon to produce Christian programmes. IMMI was a partner in fifteen special productions of *Dette er dagen* (*This is the Day*), Sunday morning services but 'adjusted for the camera'. Within three years, Eikon was nearly bankrupt. Too much hope had been placed on the long-awaited TV2. So is there a future for independent television production? Fingers have been burnt and the Church (as opposed to the missions) has little money of its own. The television companies will have to fund future programmes, and of course they will only do so if there is a market. The most positive legacy of IMMI is the Danvik *Folkehøgskole*, founded in the Danish, Grundtvig tradition. Danvik could have been, like so many others, a 'general arts' high school. It decided to concentrate entirely on media education.

KKL, in downtown Oslo, is the self-appointed watchdog of Norwegian broadcasting. It is almost as old as the state radio system. It records every minute of national TV and radio. It is an Evangelical organisation and recently mounted a campaign "by children" for "more Jesus on TV". KKL says that it makes more positive comments than negative but, perhaps naturally, it is known for its moans and groans. It began life in 1935 two years after the establishment of the broadcasting monopoly. KKL has 45,000 members. It awards scholarships to people wishing to train in communication. So far 350 scholarships have been awarded and each year a total of N.Kr.350,000 is awarded in scholarships. Another important task is media education. KKL issues 'Media with Meaning' material for adults and schools. Some time ago, KKL took over an almost equally venerable institution, the Christian Film Service. Nearly fifty per cent of Norwegian households have VCRs. The Christian Film Service believes that it has to establish a bridgehead in high street video stores. Norway has strict rules on licensing video dealerships. There is a hefty purchase tax and also a tax on cassettes. Video cassettes usually cost N.Kr220.

Eventually, of course, independent religious broadcasting on the various new broadcast channels will increase greatly. But for the next few years at least, while alternative local and satellite delivery systems continue to establish themselves, a fully-fledged public-service broadcasting system continues and indeed thrives. The *Filadelfia* Church is rather exceptional. The Norwegian local Churches and national denominations seem unwilling to grasp the challenge in a country which, for the moment and more by accident than by design, seems to enjoy the best of both worlds – a public-service system which has served the Church well, and a very free access to alternative neighbourhood broadcasting. Of course this balance will not last and slowly, especially after the creation of TV2, the weighting will shift to the disadvantage of publicly-funded broadcasting.

There are very many Norwegians who would bitterly regret a diminishment of NRK and can scarcely believe it could happen. "If religious broadcasting left the national network," says NRK's Religious Programme Officer, Gunnar Grøndahl, "they would be cutting off the branch they are sitting on." Knut Lundby, Assistant Professor in Oslo University's Department of Media and Communication, specialises in the sociology of religion. He sees a special virtue in having the national Church represented in public-service broadcasting. Norwegians are a rather private people. Many do not want their neighbours to know too much about their religious habits or convictions.

But against this, in the last hundred years, the pietistic movement has forced on everyone the question: "Are you a converted Christian?" A big majority, if forced to, would probably answer "No". However all the evidence suggests that the majority within this majority also consider Christianity to be important. It is this great group of Norwegians who are served and not condemned by public-service religious broadcasting. They are the same people whom Gunnar Grøndahl would see as his target audience. Norwegian religious culture is changing. Non-Christian faiths are now visible. The Roman Catholic Church is growing. More important still, interest in New Age religion is very marked. But the folk Church is still massive, on paper, and religious feeling is not simply skin deep. Norway is a complicated country. Many citizens would miss their 'largest Church'.

CHAPTER 10
Echo from the lake

'Shrimp' was given to me when I was nine years old. She had belonged to our doctor's son who had died in the war, very heroically, in Singapore. I owned my little ten-foot ship until she was lost in the great flood of 1953. I had to look for her mortal remains among the flotsam. I have had other small boats since that sad morning (including more 'Shrimps') but none has been quite the same. To me, she was a masterpiece. She was smooth and white and she was built 'double diagonal' which was rare even then. As often happens with our clearest memories, I have no photograph.

She had a gunter rig and even had a short bowsprit with room for two tiny foresails. But there was a problem. My father would not allow me to hoist the sails in case I ended up in Holland. For the foreseeable future and despite all my pleadings, it would have to be oars or nothing. But of course, this did not stop me stepping my mast and hauling up the Jolly Roger and on calm, hot days rowing my bare-poled galleon out to sea until the green beach huts had merged with the grassy slopes, and the black, shiny cars looked like beetles and my worried father's white, summer jacket became quite invisible.

It was out there, half a mile from shore, bobbing at anchor in the Thames Estuary, that I received my first lesson in acoustics. I could see little but I could hear everything. Motor horns, the shrieks of swimmers, dogs barking, cackling laughter, the voices of my family – they were all carried out to my floating retreat. So the loneliness was only partial. I never did discover how far away I would have to row my boat in order to find the solitude of a real ocean voyager.

All this is the reason why I have always found one particular verse in the New Testament to be so believable. Thanks to 'Shrimp', I have always been able to see the sense of it and imagine it and almost smell it. It is the opening verse of Mark's fourth chapter:

"Again Jesus began to teach beside Lake Galilee. The crowd that gathered around him was so large that he got into a boat and sat in it. The boat was out in the water, and the crowd stood on the shore at the water's edge. He used parables to teach them many things."

Jesus was at the beginning of his work. He was attracting massive attention. The crowds were very large and he could not be heard. The small boat he clambered into was not twice the size of the 'Shrimp'. Perhaps she was an off-duty fishing boat, with an anchor from her bow and with her stern tethered to a post on the shore. Perhaps she was floating free with one of the disciples holding her steady into the breeze by surreptitious pressure on the oars. The great crowd on the horseshoe beach was almost silent. As Jesus spoke to them, they could make out every word.

Jesus understood acoustics. He knew all about throwing his voice over water. Of course the boat was useful for another reason. In an earlier verse, Mark recalls one incident when the crowds by the lake grew alarmingly large. They had come from far and wide, even from Jerusalem in the South and from the Lebanon in the North. He told his disciples to get a boat ready for him so that he would not be crushed. According to Mark, Jesus went up a hill to get away. There, in the quiet, he selected the twelve apostles.

Next, Jesus went home, presumably for a rest and some privacy. But the crowds still followed him. They were so large that he could not even eat in peace. Soon he was back at the lakeside and he decided to do something about the great throng that would hardly let him move. Up to now, he had been talking to small groups of people and healing their diseases one by one. Now he dealt with the problem that seems to have almost overwhelmed him. He had to become a mass communicator. So he spoke to the crowd from the boat, bouncing his voice off the clear water of the lake.

This was the beginning of sound projection in the service of the gospel. But Jesus did not simply throw his voice in a creative manner. He also adapted what he had to say. He changed his style to meet the new situation. When he began to teach the crowd from the boat, he spoke in a way that would hold the attention of the largest number of people. His way of mass communication, and still the best broadcasting method, was to seek an unspoken response and an echo in the mind of every hearer. Now that he had moved away from a one-to-one situation, he adapted the content of his message. Standing in the boat (I think he had to be standing with his back to the breeze!), he grabbed and held the attention of the great crowd. He told his first parable, a story about the patron of all broadcasters, The Sower.

And now, twenty centuries later, the lake remains but the boats are bigger. There are tourist boats now. They chug out from Tiberias, depositing their passengers at a kibbutz for a lunch of St. Peter's Fish... and chips. The boats are fitted with their own amplifiers so that tour guides and pilgrim prelates can be heard against the wind. Throughout these two thousand years, the words of the man who knew so well this boisterous little inland sea have been told and re-told. Saints and salesman, explorers, missionaries and ordinary people have carried the Galilean's parables to every land. Sound still bounces off water but now the process seems strangely out of date. In the twentieth century there has emerged a new technology and, more significantly, a new technique for circulating the words of men. Now radio waves are reflected from the ionosphere. Since Marconi, sound, voice, ideas, information and pictures can be transmitted over the horizon to faraway receivers.

Today's world is full of broadcasting. For most of the century, sowers in five continents have been scattering their electronic seed. The true novelty of this procedure is not technical but behavioural. One class of human beings has learned the special techniques of one-way communication. The media men have discovered how to squeeze the human persona through broadcasting's peculiar non-return valve. The remainder of the species has readily adapted to a receptive role. The parable from the boat has been given a bizarre, secular meaning. "He that has ears (or FM stereo or a satellite dish) to hear, let him hear."

The planet has become an ever-noisier Babel and the noise has had a powerful effect. Once it was religion that defined our values and our culture. Now countries and social systems are freshly glued together by broadcasting. It provides our information and determines our worldview. It unifies our accents and our language. It pictures our fantasies and provides our escapes. Broadcasting fixes our stereotypes. Even our monarchs have been forced to become its stars.

The effect on the human race has been stupendous. We have not only developed mass communications. We have also let a powerful genie out of the cathode ray tube. Now we have in our midst a technology combined with a technique that can change our perception of reality. If broadcasting could be distilled and put back in its bottle, it would belong on the same shelf as alcohol. Even when it is used with the best of intentions, broadcasting can do amazing things to our brain cells. Like alcohol, it will not go away. Perhaps, like alcohol, it should at all times be handled with caution. Christians in particular, whose core belief is that the Word became flesh, must take note of a health warning: "Broadcasting can seriously damage the flesh."

In *1984*, George Orwell describes a population numbed and marshalled by orders barked from loudspeakers on every street corner. In one respect his prophecy has come true. There really is a mind-bending machine in every living room. But, as Neil Postman reminds us, it is Aldous Huxley's prophecy that has been more accurately fulfilled. Our machine was not padlocked to the wall by the Thought Police. We put it there ourselves. We do not shuffle up to it like doped, mind-blown zombies. We run to it eagerly and happily to bask in its technicolour glow. It has become the opium of the people and few of us would deny it our devotions.

We speak of mass communication but, notwithstanding Pierre Babin, the word 'communicate' has been stripped of two-thirds of its meaning. Perhaps it should not do so but nowadays, it simply means to impart. Notions of 'sharing' and 'participation' have been blown away. The new communication is a delivery into thin air in the expectation that not everything will fall among tares. If those with ears to hear are indeed listening, the communicator will never know, at least not until his colleague, the audience researcher, has gone to work.

Even as the neo-communicators seek to impart and stimulate, their freedom of expression is heavily constrained. Neo-communicators cannot simply borrow a boat or a soap box and then hold their crowd in a personal magnetic field. Mass communication is expensive and the broadcaster is only permitted to sow his seed after a huge number of media requirements have been satisfied. When Jesus spoke from the boat, there needed to be no commercial breaks to pay for the boat. The boat was provided without fee (at least I would be very disappointed if it wasn't!) and the water which acted as such an effective sound-mirror was free also. No-one had to pay for seats or for a receiving licence in that natural amphitheatre. In other words the delivery system, if that is what it was, came free as air.

It has been put more than once by radioactive Christians that if God had only left it another two thousand years before his Word became flesh, then the message of salvation would have been brought to us electronically. This is an impossible idea to develop. It is like worrying about whether or not there are intelligent lobsters on other planets who are capable of unselfish love. There are many things we will never know. God made the appointment. He chose the time and the place. Indeed it might be considered further evidence of his infinite wisdom that he scrupulously avoided any involvement with the mass media.

But not everyone is against the idea of God making personal use of the broadcasting industry. "Jesus would have used television", says Piet Derksen. "For the Sermon on the Mount he stood on a little hillock." Some Christians in the media have practiced two-hop satellite links with the Mount of Olives. They were limbering up for the end of the age. They are putting the hardware in place for the greatest interview of all time! The Son of God on television! Would he or wouldn't he? So many of Christ's personality tracks are covered. We know nothing about his face or his voice or his height or his mannerisms or his preferences or his hobbies. We are left with living words and deeds and just enough of a *curriculum vitae* to hang them on. Could a video-tape add one iota to our salvation history?

Perhaps Jesus would have avoided the electronic media but that does not necessarily mean that his disciples have to do the same. Nevertheless we cannot forget that the core of the Christian

122

religion is participation. There can be no 'TV football', no 'radio sex'. These terms are self-contradictory. What broadcasting can do is to show us, through its unblinking and collective eye, the exciting things that other people are doing. Broadcasting can stimulate us and suggest to us. It is a spectator sport. The service that it never provides, but which, nevertheless, it constantly strives to replicate, is shared human contact.

Every television picture is by definition second-hand. The eye that selects each picture is not my eye. Everything that is broadcast is edited and already chosen, if only by the cameraman. There can be no Electronic Church. The reason for this is not simply found in the nature of broadcasting itself but in the nature of God. Of course there can be plenty of news coverage and editorialising about the Easter message. But when the Word becomes mere words, he cannot dwell anywhere. The Word became flesh. He was not a disembodied word.

Jesus Christ communicated within real flesh-and-blood relationships. He could be felt and touched even after his Resurrection. Would he have been seen dead on television? Even if he had been seen alive after Good Friday, would the sight of him convince one viewer? One of the realities of television is that it develops its own credibility gap. Would Thomas have believed a close-up video-recording of the wounded hands and side? Marshall McLuhan left us his much-quoted aphorism "The medium is the message" and he left us much else besides. Neil Postman, a McLuhan disciple, prefers a development of the McLuhan theme: "The medium is the metaphor". Perhaps, in one sense, the Word of God is the message. More certainly, he is the metaphor of God. Above all, he is the medium – the means for a great transaction.

So, should Christ's disciples run the serious risk of broadcasting? Certainly they may. First-century Palestine was a culturally-mixed and highly-commercialised land. The gospels mean little if they are not tales of peril, exposure and nakedness. There were many failures. Obviously, Christian broadcasting cannot be a 'great loudspeaker'. Nearly every Christian broadcaster would nowadays agree that he must not become a religiously-minded Captain Queeg, grabbing the first available microphone for a "Now hear this" to the human race. But broadcasting is never what it seems. It is the foolish Christian who runs cock-a-hoop through the studio door. An urge to show forth the love of the Lord is not enough. There are many trip-switches that make radio and, above all television, work in ways that no-one has planned.

Speaking at the 1988 Lambeth Conference and not ten miles from where I voyaged in my 'Shrimp', Father Pierre Duprey, Secretary of the Vatican Council for Promoting Christian Unity[1], re-stated the need to hear properly: "Today, the mind of Christians, whatever their role in the Church, risks increasingly being formed by television, radio and the press, rather than by our receiving and pondering the Word of God which is heard and celebrated in the Church. What is the danger here? The danger is that the newness given in Christ, the newness that is operative in and through the Church may be discerned only with difficulty, and perhaps with greater difficulty than was the case in the past. The risk we run is that the organisation of the Community, of the society of the Church, its various services and ministries... will be coloured and influenced by the currents and the thoughts of the present world. Our vision and understanding risks being shaped by the spirit of this world, a spirit which runs counter to the Spirit of God."

References

[1] Father Duprey was responding to the Archbishop of Canterbury on "The Nature of the Unity We Seek". July 19th, 1988.

CHAPTER 11

Drielandenpunt

In past centuries, all media were religious. Christianity was expressed through painting, poetry, drama and architecture. The creative artist, whether he was an icon painter or a musician, was highly valued. Art was not decoration. It was essential to theological and liturgical expression. Christian communication must now escape from iconoclasm. The great need is for a new creativity. Technology is not a problem. At least technological problems can be solved. For the right idea finance can be found. The complaint of producers is that they are looking in vain to the Church for ideas and for a pool of creative people. Many of the ideas that Christians put forward are unusable because they fail to appreciate the delicacy of the medium. The British Council of Churches had a special committee which provided seed money to finance proposals or 'treatments' for religious TV programmes on Britain's Channel 4. None of the treatments was accepted. The Churches should ask themselves why this was so.

The Church must again search out and value her creative artists. This can begin in school, college, congregation and in the mini-media of dance and mime. Christian broadcasters must first of all be self-expressive. They face huge pressures – from management, peer group and from Church. They must be allowed to satisfy their own integrity. Some Christians in the media are altogether too religious. Or they are what the broadcaster and teacher Michael Shoesmith calls "Arminians at heart". They think that "It all depends on me" and "I have to change the world". One of the great benefits of the multiplication of channels and the consequent increase of narrowcasting is that expectations will become more realistic. Some pressures will be reduced.

TRAINING THE TRAINERS

Just at the time when Europe is experiencing such a great increase in the number of broadcasting channels, the training of Christian broadcasters is at its lowest ebb. The training problem is rooted in uncertainty about the nature of religious broadcasting. A European Broadcast Training Association would be a useful first step. It must span the ecclesiastical spectrum, not to achieve a warm inclusive glow, but for a much more down-to-earth reason. If this wide-angle perspective is not achieved, such an association would fail in its purpose. An entirely new institution is required. It must not be captured by any Church, interdenominational institution, academic discipline or communication theory. The habits of half a lifetime must be broken. An ecumenical agenda (hidden, overt or understood) must be specifically written out of the constitution. The idea is not to achieve a synthesis but to discuss, disseminate and hold in creative tension the widest possible range of communication ideologies.

Public-service cuts have made professional training less available. Communication Studies and indeed training can be made to mean practically anything. Anyone, from any background, can now be a broadcasting trainer. The Church's own training is too often far from rigorous. A medium-term solution would be for a number of European universities to provide serious courses for the accreditation of senior peripatetic trainers.

TRAINING FULL-TIME BROADCASTERS

Training should be provided for Eastern Europeans but *only* as a result of their own specific requests and initiatives and *only* on a country-by-country basis. In Western Europe, there has been, for many years, a considerable number of inter-media courses. Unsurprisingly, in the countries where the Church has owned its own newspapers and radio stations, these training courses are more developed. Spain has two universities solely devoted to preparation for work in the mass media. In the Nordic countries, there are a number of media Folk High Schools where the emphasis is less on handling electronic hardware. The aim is to develop communicating people. The Swedish Pentecostal Church has made monumental efforts in general media training. In France, *CREC-AVEX* has launched a new French-English course in liaison with the University of Lyon.

In those countries where public-service broadcasting systems have long held sway, the Churches' training programmes (particularly in television) have not been acceptable to the national broadcasters. Therefore, the Churches have turned their attention to providing training for Christians from overseas. Italy's Paulist order (which probably represents Christian Europe's greatest single manpower investment in the mass media) holds courses for students from many Third World countries. In the last ten years, the Churches' training institutions have also concentrated on local and community radio.

The situation is almost the same in the United States. University degree courses in journalism or media studies and the expensive Broadcasting Schools are almost the only avenues into full-time broadcasting. In fairness, it has to be said of the much-maligned Electronic Church that it has made a big contribution to broadcast training. Some of the TV preachers have the great advantage of being able to offer a combination of university education with real studio experience. Apprenticeships in Toronto with David Mainse are much sought-after. His concern for European broadcasting has been serious and long-term. Oral Roberts University in Tulsa is a fully-accredited educational institution. Its Department of Communications Studies has trained a number of Europeans. At a 1990 meeting in Munich, far away from Virginia Beach, plans were discussed for a European offshoot of Pat Robertson's Regent University.

As public-service broadcasting contracts, there will be a training vacuum. It is sad that this unfilled niche, so obvious to North America's missionary-minded TV preachers, does not seem to greatly concern the European Churches. An ecumenical response might simply be another excuse for wasting time. Urgent and, if necessary, unilateral action is required. As this book is being completed, the Robert Schuman Institute of Journalism and European Media Studies opens in Brussels. It is based on the same firm convictions about the continent and about training. Europe, the cradle of modern civilisation, cannot build itself up without training people. "The Christian way of understanding events is an integral part of training." The Schuman Institute chairman is Willy Boers, a Director of Piet Derksen's Foundation for the Witnessing of God's Love.

TRAINING LOCAL BROADCASTERS

'Local' means different things in different countries. The city-wide television coverage in parts of Sweden is local. So are Norway's ten-watt stations or the myriad low-powered community services that, in the last ten years, have sprung up across Europe. In every case the listener is unforgiving. Aunt Betty in Jutland makes no distinctions. Radio must sound like radio. On the whole, and because the opportunities have been obvious to all, the Churches have made a serious training response to truly local broadcasting.

Christians are among the greatest non-commercial users of VCRs. Video training has long been available in many countries and this has provided the jumping-off point for religious broadcasting on cable. In community-access television, there are many cases of Church-based video groups providing training for less experienced political or local action organisations. Some form of local radio training has been provided by most of the major Christian groups. But there has been a certain amount of consumer resistance. People become disappointed when, after going through a training course, they then discover that they are not in the charmed circle and that no-one requires them to broadcast. Too many courses assume that the highest form of life is to sit in front of a microphone. Much more emphasis must be placed on training for radio's essential technical and support services. Also there needs to be a much greater co-ordination of training on a national level. Too many religious-training initiatives have sprouted like mushrooms for what are, after all, nationally regulated systems. Far too many unqualified people and institutions have set themselves up as trainers and clearing houses.

It has been said, perhaps unkindly, of the BBC's local radio service, that it is held together by 'part-time Anglican vicars'. 'Part-time' is an unkind cut, not to the BBC but to the vicars! People become broadcasters in a great variety of ways. There is no single route to the studio chair. The attractive and fluid nature of local broadcasting tempts the practitioners to undervalue their own skills and experience. In some cases their own professional associations and self-help groups admit to membership anyone who is prepared to pay a subscription. This debases the coinage. Ways must be found for highly-skilled and senior local broadcasters to be more highly valued, not only by their Churches but by themselves.

TRAINING VIEWERS AND LISTENERS

There is widespread agreement that consumers need to analyse television. At its simplest, this means monitoring the broadcast output and applying pressure on politicians and broadcasters. Norway's KKL is one of Europe's oldest media watchdogs. The Christian monitoring groups tend to take the position that quality television is possible but that standards must be maintained.

Media Awareness goes deeper. It involves understanding the overall effect of broadcasting on our individual perceptions and social values. Media Awareness began in the United States. It is the offspring of the conviction of many liberal American researchers that television may be hazardous. A number of mainline American Churches run comprehensive Media Awareness training programmes. The Television Awareness Training programme (TAT) of the the United Methodist Church was one of the first. A current leader in the field is California-based *Media and Values*.

Media Awareness training is on the agenda of some European Churches. In the German Evangelical Church, there is a hard-headed and special emphasis on training Church leaders. The Church of Sweden's programme on media effects is arranged under four headings: medical, social, sociological and psychological. An English inter-Church media awareness programme is sponsored by the Mothers' Union. In Italy there is a collective emphasis. Umberto Eco's semiotic guerillas may not have arrived yet but very many parishes have facilities for evaluating films and videos. The Jesuits of the EDAV centre in La Spezia run courses and publish the country's leading magazine on the effects of everything from pin-ups to the news. Sweden is one country which requires Media Awareness to be a compulsory part of the school curriculum. The first of several laws was passed in 1962. To assess the situation, a Stockholm researcher, Karen Stigbrand, sent a detailed questionnaire to 700 teachers. Media Awareness seems to have been 'one good idea too many'. Current regulations are not enforced. According to Karen Stigbrand, who now directs *Kabelnämden*, the Swedish Cable Authority, Ministry of Education officials are "conscious of a weak point".

In both America and Europe, Media Awareness has to be understood as a very broad term. Some researchers believe that it will always be impracticable to inoculate enough viewers by education. Others believe that television itself ought to be compelled to carry its own inbuilt remedy or health warning, rather as fluoride is put into drinking water or cautions are printed on cigarette advertising. Neil Postman half-seriously suggests that TV programmes which parody themselves may be an answer. Many writers, including Postman and Huxley, echo H.G.Wells that we have limited options. Human beings are in a race between education and disaster.

PROGRAMME MAKING

The greatest single need in European broadcasting is for new programmes. This is going to be equally true for Christian broadcasting. Of course in many cases, high-quality religious programmes will continue to be made. Public-service broadcasting will not disappear overnight. A German commentator, Georg-Michael Luyken, believes that the next phase in the story of the European audio-visual industry may include a groundswell press-ure for more quality programming.

The national corporations will be increasingly open to independently-produced programmes. In Britain, the requirement is that twenty-five per cent should be provided by independent companies. Britain's Independent Programme Providers Association (IPPA) has about 600 members. Alan Sapper of ACTT believes that no more than eighty of these are "real" and that perhaps "only six to a dozen are well-established". "If you need three thousand hours of programming a year, how are you going to fill a schedule?" Alan Sapper believes that the independents will simply be swallowed up by TV conglomerates.

However, in their different ways, Britain's Channel 4 and Germany's EDF have relied successfully on independently-produced material. In some countries, this has been a long tradition of effective independent religious production. In the Netherlands there is the renowned *Ikon* production house. In Germany there is the much smaller Eikon of Munich. ERF in Wetzlar is an evangelical producer, outside the orbit of the German Evangelical Church. *Evangeliums Rundfunk* has been built up around alternative transmission systems. It has a mailing list of a quarter of a million, 150 employees and an annual budget of DM 20 million.

The new openings in the traditional broadcast channels, combined with limited opportunities by satellite and rather more on cable, offer an inescapable challenge to religious broadcasters. Pentecostal Christians in particular, and a broad group of the so-called 'new denominations', house fellowships and Restorationists are making detailed plans and major financial investments. Their success will depend on their ability to make viewable programmes. If the American experience means anything, they will have some success. The morale of hitherto invisible religious groups is greatly lifted by broadcasting. For a number of reasons so-called para-Churches have most to gain from media exposure. The question for the longer-established Churches is whether they too must make a direct response. "Who will be the programme makers?" Faced with a diminishing presence on the airwaves, will the churches themselves drum up enough money to pay for their own production and marketing enterprises?

The stand-off between the Churches of Northern Europe and national broadcasting has not pleased every Christian. Nevertheless successful broadcasting requires a degree of detachment. Viewers remain unconvinced when everyone on the screen is a supporter. In programmes directly controlled and paid for by the Church, controversial issues would be avoided. Programmes would be little better than those of the Californian Televangelist who is simultaneously the owner, the producer and, with his glamorous wife, the presenter – all rolled into one. Most Church synods have problems enough understanding the subtleties of broadcasting. If as well as having to find understanding, they also had to find cash, there would be no end to the arguments. "No," says John Barton, former Chief Broadcasting Officer of the Church of England. "If the churches do try to make programmes, they will produce just enough money for the enterprises to be a disaster."

If there is to be a mainstream religious presence in the new broadcasting channels, it will have to be detached and distanced from the Churches. Again the North American experience is instructive. In Catholic North America, it is the religious orders rather than the dioceses who are making waves. After many frustrations and false dawns, the mainline Churches have found a new and surprisingly effective channel in the new VISN InterFaith Network. Positioning is all-important. Experience in programme-making must be undertaken long before particular channels become available. Europe's Churches can do much to support, sponsor and stimulate. Very few independent producers are financially secure. They have to be underwritten by charitable foundations, as in the case of Denmark's KKR or England's CTVC, or, in the words of Barrie Allcott, CTVC's director, they can hope to "stumble over a blockbuster". While waiting for new openings in television, a much smaller English production house, Dales TV has concentrated on building up its general business activities.

A one-hour documentary requires at least £15,000 to research but only a small number of national churches are willing to make direct grants. In 1989 the Church of Sweden devoted S.Kr.200,000 to programme production. Subsidies do not always have to be speculative. Ideally, funds can be granted to a producer who has already been promised an airing. One of the most serious problems, which affects religious and secular producers alike, is the question of copyright. More often than not, producers cede their rights in order to gain one, or perhaps two, screenings. The Churches should support national measures which strengthen and protect the smaller producers. One imaginative proposal is the Hilversum-based Eurolynk. Using satellite distribution, the point of the scheme is to make Europe's scheduling managers more aware of a range of Christian and secular programmes. It aims to assist the ninety-five per cent of productions that are not shown at television festivals.

It is always true that Churches should avoid investing in their own broadcast hardware. It can be comforting to show off a studio full of expensive equipment or point to a gleaming roof-top up-link dish. European and American Churches have invested great sums in expensive studios that have turned out to be white elephants. The names of Mainz and Chicago still send shudders down the spines of Church accountants. As a rule of thumb, religious producers should, until the last possible moment, hire equipment and expertise.

A far more useful investment by the national Churches would be to give substantial cash prizes for outstanding religious programmes. In the United States, the Paulist Fathers make the annual Humanitas Award of $25,000. For many years there have been a number of prestigious European awards. Based in Neuchâtel, the *Prix Farel* offers a commemorative glass and S.Fr.1,000. The German Evangelical Church has the Robert Geisendorfer prize of DM 7,000 and a medal. Sadly, in recent years, a number of meaningless broadcasting 'awards' have been scattered like confetti across Europe. However, real money would soon reverse this devaluation. Quite apart from the question of kudos, a sum that could give financial security to a script-writer for six or nine months would certainly be a solid encouragement for more religious themes to be tackled.

TRANS-BORDER PRODUCTION

Ecumenism and the end-of-century march towards European unity both lead many Christian producers to a recurring question. Is it not time for countries to meet? Could Christians from different countries pool resources and see the continent as a whole? Is it not true that the European audio-visual industry needs to free itself from American domination. At the same time, some Churchmen are fearing an influx of hot-gospel Televangelism. Is this not a case of "Divided we fall"? Could there not be programmes which would remind Europeans of their Christian roots, restore their broken unity, share the high costs of production and, all at the same time, help in the Brussels drive to fight off the Americans? There are, of course, trans-border productions already. Robert Schuller's *Hour of Power* comes just as it is to Europe's skies. In his heyday, Jimmy Swaggart had one of the greatest lip-sync departments in the world but dubbing cannot remove what some Americans have called the "culture-bound material". Therefore a very great deal of the world's evangelistic television is rooted in the American worldview which, partly because of television itself, knows no frontiers.

So should there be a European joint response? Is market fragmentation a real problem for European Christian broadcasters? Some producers are emphatic. Dr. Renate Maiocchi, who directs the Italian Protestant programme on RAI, would find a European desk very valuable. He has support among Swiss, Belgian and Dutch broadcasters. There are occasions when archive material, film clips and complete programmes are required. A clearing-house would make this possible and keep down costs. However, programme makers in the larger television markets are more relaxed. At present they have adequate facilities.

The European Ecumenical Satellite Committee, believes that the time has come for trans-border productions to be investigated. EESC believes that co-production will become a key word for Europe's religious programme makers but that it will be hard to find funding-partners and that language-barriers remain a major difficulty. Language is only one aspect of wider cultural and national problems. In some countries, notably France, these problems may be insurmountable. Even a commonly-held Catholic heritage may not be enough to interest a French viewer in an Italian programme. In the centre of the new Europe, in Germany, there is more optimism. The Germans, who practise a kind of public-service narrowcasting, have a liking for religious program-mes with a magazine format. This might be the best way to handle Euro-religion. On the outer fringes of Europe, the Portuguese, the British and the Swedes have less enthusiasm.

In 1967, Aubrey Singer's *Our World*, which looked for shared values, was taken off the BBC after one showing. However, European likes and dislikes are changing very fast and should not transfix the Churches. There are some religious themes which would surely interest a wide audience. Norman Stone's *Martin Luther, Heretic* would touch a chord in many countries. Trans-border productions might have to be heavy on action to get over the language problem. Alternatively, there would have to be major investments in language dubbing. Television stunts and hook-ups have possibilities but they are unrepeatable. European social problems could be a rich source of common understanding. Producers must be aware of the difficulties of working across frontiers but not necessarily put off by them. They may be called to be trend-setters.

OWNERSHIP

"I'm not in the communication business. I'm only a Church of Scotland minister." These unfortunate words were indiscreet enough to be overheard. They could have been uttered anywhere in Europe and in any Church. Too often Christians have convinced themselves that communication is somehow 'modern'; that there is a new class of expert who holds the keys to its special secrets. For inexplicable reasons, the Church has developed an inferiority complex vis-à-vis the media. The result is the newly-blind pleading to be led by the long-term blind. Churches have been more concerned for their own place on the airwaves than for broadcasting as a whole. In this respect the reputation of Scottish churchmen can be immediately restored. A delegation travelled south to London on March 19th, 1990 for a meeting about Britain's new broadcasting legislation. Afterwards they said, "We made it clear that our interest was first in the matter of quality programmes in general, second in the Scottish dimension and thirdly in religious broadcasting."

But Christians are rarely neutral about public-service broadcasting. Dave Adams, European Director of Trans World Radio, speaks of an earlier German situation: "People couldn't hear echoes of their own religious convictions. Public broadcasting failed to reflect diversity. There was not enough capacity for different points of view." A rather different opinion is stated by Archdeacon John Barton. "Britain has something of which it can be really proud. But religious programmes in public-service broadcasting are not *reaping* activities. On the other hand, they may sometimes be *sowing* activities." Father Pasquale Borgomeo makes an unexpected confession: "To some extent we at Vatican Radio are much more independent from what is generally regarded as religious".

Christians have different views of broadcasting history. At different stages various religious groups have felt excluded. They have prayed for the chains to be broken. In the early days in Britain, Catholics certainly resented the BBC's rather bland religion. Until the end of the war Protestants were excluded from Italian radio. In most public-service systems, most Evangelicals have felt cold-shouldered by most liberal Protestant establishments. Nowadays Evangelicals are far stronger and have the powerful support of a transatlantic alliance. The broadcasting monopolies have been broken and new media openings are at last available. In the meantime many otherwise-vocal Christians, both Protestant and Catholic, are quite silent on the one issue that really concerns lawmakers and the general public. Broadcasting freedom will solve all problems. "You can rely on us," they assure us, "the worst excesses of the United States will never come to Europe. As for the gospel, it will stand on its own two feet and see off all the competition from other faiths and none". Up to now, some European governments have been less than certain that this optimism is justified.

There is much talk of ownership of stations. In Spain, Portugal and Italy, there is talk of networks. In Protestant, Catholic and Charismatic Europe, there are dreams of Christian satellite channels. The debate about ownership is, in fact, a diversion. If ownership means possession, it guarantees nothing. It matters not who owns a broadcasting facility. The really important factors are programming freedom and audience size. Missionary radio has known this for years. Trans World Radio and Sweden's IBRA rent airtime on other people's transmitters. Nevertheless, the conviction persists that if only Christians could at least own the media, all kinds of benefits would follow. Ownership would allow a straightforward expression of faith and a continent could be won back for Christ. Other evangelistic Christians entertain some doubts. "Culture has moved away and so the gospel is incomprehensible," says Dave Adams in an echo of the British missiologist Lesslie Newbiggin. "There has to be a fundamental paradigm shift. The only possible justification for Christians running their own service is to provide an environment for testing and working through the presentation of a Christian worldview."

The evidence is increasingly clear. Even if ownership guarantees control, which in turn guarantees free expression, there is still no guarantee of an audience. Who then is in control? Communicators have to obey not only their controllers but also the laws of their medium. The Christian gospel cannot simply be picked up and transmitted as a Shannon and Weaver message. When this is done, almost nothing happens. One of the intriguing facets of researching your own station's audience is that everyone else's dirty

136

washing is revealed at the same time. Therefore the research department of the BBC World Service knows a very great number of embarrassing facts about the number of listeners to missionary radio in, for instance, Eastern Europe. It is absolutely clear that only the short-wave stations who schedule their religious programmes as part of a diverse range of programmes have any measurable audience. All-religious channels get nowhere.

Confirmation of this comes from the wrongly-designated Televangelists of the United States. They, at least, can be said to display intelligence and discrimination in their use of media. In their *printed* appeals for prayer partners and financial support, the tone is urgent. The times are evil and the end of the age is drawing near. The donor base of supporters and subscribers is urged to give generously and to participate in calling the world to repentance. However, in their *television* appearances to the general public, the message is one of humour and family values, success and sexual attractiveness. The big preaching stars with their own day-long schedules very sensibly offer a diverse range of programmes. Without a haircut, John the Baptist would not get even one sound-bite. Calls to repentance are at least equalled in number by old *Lassie* movies.

Religious broadcasting on its own simply does not win a congregation. Confirmation of this basic finding comes from many quarters. In 1990, the Catholic producers of America's VISN Network received a detailed report on the future of Christian broadcasting. In audience terms, there is no future for purely religious television. There is, however, a considerable market opportunity for broadly-based 'values oriented' programming. It may well be that, in Northern Europe, the broadcasting products of the liberal Protestant ascendancy are rejected. But the wheel will eventually come full circle. Whatever emerges as a replacement will simply be an Evangelical version of the same well-proven format. If Christian broadcasting is to be public and not simply preaching to the converted, it has to be in a diverse, as well as a diverting, setting. Perhaps the internecine Christian strife has not been about content at all. The problem has been caused less by *what* various Christians broadcast. It has more to do with *which* Christians do the broadcasting.

*

DRIELANDENPUNT

It is a commonplace that, whenever the Church feels that a gap has opened and needs to be plugged, a specialist is appointed. Youth workers, industrial chaplains, fund-raisers, inner-city ministers, are all appointed as counter-measures to cure some of the Church's famous weaknesses. Communication must not be treated in this way! In most European countries, the Churches have communication specialists at national and regional levels. Finland has information chiefs, the Church of Scotland has forty-seven presbytery publicity officers, most Church of England dioceses have communication officers – some of them full-time. In West Germany, Protestants, Evangelicals and Catholics have impressive communication institutions. In the religious orders and in most European countries, certainly at the level of the national conferences of bishops, the Roman Catholic Church has an impressive array of specialists and advisers. The problem is everywhere the same. Communication is rightly perceived as a special crisis area for the Christian Church. *Unreasonably*, the problem is handed to the care of a specialist. But communication is not a category of the Church's activity (like fund-raising or inner-city mission). Communication is everything and the Bible is the record of God's communication. In the words of Cardinal Martini of Milan, "the Church *is* Communication' and it is the bishop (or the moderator or the superintendent or whoever) who is the President of Communication.

The final 'illustration' in my album is of a real place in our holiday memories. Years ago, when the children were small, we spent an hour or two at the *Drielandenpunt*, the Dutch name for the place where Germany, Belgium and the Netherlands all meet. There is a fine view over Aachen but the *raison d'être* for the carpark and the ice-creams is the unpretentious obelisk where the three frontiers come together. Our half-Dutch children felt they deserved a place in the *Guinness Book of Records*. In a quarter of an hour, they had visited Germany and Belgium more than a hundred times! We took it in turns to sit on top of the *Drielandenpunt* monument. In this position, of course, we were in three countries at once. And that is just where the Europe's Christian communication needs to be based.

A shepherd by many other names, the Christian strategist must stand on his very own *drielandenpunt*. The Church itself is, by definition, the homeland. Each medium of communication is a new territory, with its own signs and language. But to stand at the interface of Church and medium is not enough. Indeed, such a positioning often results in communication disaster. When Christians have spied new media, they have too often acted exploitatively and not as media ecologists. Christian communication needs to stand on three legs.

So there exists a third dimension, fully equal to the other two. This is the dimension of intelligent humility, where insight is sought into how it is that we create our meanings. This does not have to be Communication Studies. That smacks of complexity and, in any case, this science cannot be said with confidence to exist. Intelligent humility is for anyone who can ponder the possibilities, and therefore the limitations, inherent in every medium. If, as Cardinal Martini claims, "the Church is Communication", there has to be a new confidence and clarity of purpose. Communication will first be distinguished (far away from the electronic media) in personal and family relationships. The Church will begin to draw more rigorous distinctions between evangelisation, public relations and befriending. Media will be seen collectively and there will no longer be an over-reliance on broadcasting. The Church's communication crisis will not be solved by more specialists or more media. Communication is Everything. Therefore it is everyone's business. Broadcasting has its proper place. It is, if you like, a speciality. But as such it is but a tiny part of the whole. In seminaries and colleges, communication will not be seen as just another option. No longer will it be confused with amateur radio.

Responsibility for Christian communication must not be dodged. The buck stops with the one who aspires to be the servant of the servants. In the vital area of policy making, and especially in the making and monitoring of appointments, it is the President of Communication himself whose task it is, *not* to delegate to communication experts, still less to abdicate to those with hands-on experience, but to seek personal enlightenment and to analyse his own use of every medium; to adjust, to steer and to fine-tune. He will consider all media and, at the same time, he will be discriminating and allocate resources. He may well conclude that small is beautiful. His task will never be completed. He applies a steady but variable pressure to keep the three legs of the Christian communication tripod in continuous contact with the ground.

Bibliography

Five books are referred to in the text:-

The McBride Report
MANY VOICES, ONE WORLD
Report by the International
Commission for the Study of
Communication Problems
Published, in association with
WACC, by
Kogan Page/Unipub/UNESCO
(1980)
ISBN 0 85038 348 X

Communio e progressio
The Pastoral Instruction for the
application of the decree of the
Second Vatican Ecumenical
Council on the means of Social
Communication
Catholic Truth Society

AMUSING OURSELVES TO
DEATH
Neil Postman
Methuen (1985)
ISBN 0 413 40440 4

REALLY BAD NEWS
Glasgow Media Group
Writers and Readers Publishing
Cooperative Society (1982)
ISBN 0 906495 44 X

GODWATCHING
Viewers, Religion and Television.
Michael Svennevig, Ian Haldane,
Sharon Spiers, Barrie Gunter.
John Libbey (1988)
086 196 199 4

The following books have been my
travelling companions:-

LET THE EARTH HEAR
Paul E. Freed
Nelson (1980)
ISBN 0 8407 5729 8
(The story of one of major missionary radios)

THE CHURCHES AND THE
BRITISH BROADCASTING
CORPORATION
1922–1956
The Politics of Broadcast Religion
Kenneth M. Wolfe
SCM Press (1984)
ISBN 334 01932 X

CHRISTIAN
COMMUNICATION
RECONSIDERED
John Bluck
World Council of Churches (1989)
ISBN 2 8254 0975 8

ADVERTISING AS
COMMUNICATION
Gillian Dyer
Routledge (1982)
ISBN 0 415 02781 0
(Especially Chapter Six on 'Semiotics and ideology')

MYTHMAKERS
Gospel, Culture and the Media
William F. Fore
Friendship Press, New York
(1990)
ISBN 0 377 00207 0

The Cecchini Report
THE EUROPEAN
CHALLENGE
1992
Wildwood House
ISBN 0 7045 0613 0

EUROPE 2000:
What Kind of Television
The Report of the European
Television Task Force
The European Institute for the
Media (1988)
ISBN 0948195 17 7

THE FUTURE OF THE
EUROPEAN AUDIOVISUAL
INDUSTRY
André Lange and Jean-Luc
Renaud
The European Institute for the
Media (1989)
ISBN 0 948195 15 0

COHERENCE IN DIVERSITY:
The Challenge for European
Television
The European Institute for the
Media (1990)
ISBN 0 948195 25 8

TELEVISION IN 1992
A Guide to Europe's New TV,
Film and Video Business
John Howkins and Michael Foster
Coopers & Lybrand (1990)

MASS MEDIA RELIGION
The Social Sources of the
Electronic Church
Stewart M. Hoover (1988)
Sage
ISBN 0 8039 2995 1

Sadly, Dr. Ingmar Lindqvist's
*DELADE MENINGAR, OM
KOMMUNIKATION OCH
VERKLIGHET* (Disagreements on
Communication and Reality) is
presently available in Swedish only.
I possess a Swedish manuscript but
100 per cent of my understanding
of its contents comes from
conversations and correspondence
with the author.

I have made use of the following
articles and papers:-

CONCEPTS OF RELIGIOUS
BROADCASTING IN BBC
RADIO, 1922–1987 Ove
Ingvaldstad. A thesis presented to
the English Department of the
University of Trondheim. Spring
1989.

VIEWER AWARENESS
STUDY. Conducted by ASI
MARKET RESEARCH Inc for
the Catholic VISN Producers, San
Francisco. November 6th 1989.

COMMUNICATIONS AND
RESEARCH TRENDS
A Quarterly Information Service
from the Centre for the Study of
Communication and Culture,
London
(The complete set from Spring
1980 onwards)

COMMUNICATION AND
EVANGELISATION IN
EUROPE
Robert A. White SJ
Centre for the Study of
Communication and Culture,
London (August 1988)

SEMINARIUM
Instrumenta communicationis socialis in formatione sacerdotali. No. 4. Libraria Editrice Vaticana. October–December 1986.

CRITERIA FOR ECUMENICAL AND INTER-RELIGIOUS COOPERATION IN COMMUNICATIONS
Pontifical Council for Social Communications. Vatican City 1989.

RELIGION IN RADIO AND TV DURING SIXTY YEARS.
Dr. Rune Larsson's English summary of his book.

LES RITES ET LA TÉLÉVISION.
Guy Martinot SJ
Vie consacrée 1989. No. 6.

TARGETING THE AUDIENCE
The text of the speech by Graham Mytton, Head of International Broadcasting and Audience Research, BBC World Service, to European Religious Broadcasters 1990.

A RATIONALE FOR RELIGIOUS COMMUNICATION.
Dr. Chris Arthur
Centre for Theology and Public Issues, New College, Edinburgh.

In *WERELD EN ZENDING, Oecumenisch tijdschrift voor missiologie en missionaire praktijk, voor Nederland en België*, 1989 No. 3, there is, in Dutch, an assessment of *Lumen 2,000* by Lejo Schenk and Aaltje van Valderen.

THE AUDIO-VISUAL MEDIA IN THE SINGLE EUROPEAN MARKET
Office for the Official Publications of the European Communities.
Luxembourg
ISBN 92 825 8403 8

THE COMMUNITY'S BROADCASTING POLICY
Office for the Official Publications of the European Communities.
Luxembourg
ISBN 92 825 6501 7

143

Acknowledgments

I am grateful to the following for their time and for their insights.

Herr Stephan Abarbanell, German Evangelical Church, Frankfurt

Mr. Dave Adams, Trans World Radio, Hilversum

Rev. Barrie Allcott, CTVC,

Mr. Ross Anderson, Church of Scotland

Rev. Loyse Andrée, *Télévision Suisse Romande*, Geneva

Ed Arons, Lumen 2000, Eindhoven

Professor Sigbert Axelsson, University of Uppsala

Père Pierre Babin, CREC-AVEX, Lyon

Rev. Jon Baldvinsson, Icelandic Embassy, London

The Very Rev. Professor Robin Barbour, Church of Scotland

Rev. Chris Bard, EON

Mr. Andrew Barr, TVS

The Ven. John Barton, former Chief Broadcasting Officer, Church of England

Rev. David Beer, Anglia Television

Belfast Independent Video

Mr. Eddy Blackwell, Independent Local Radio, U.K.

Father Pasquale Borgomeo SJ, Vatican Radio

Mr. Lyndon Bowring, CARE Trust

Rev Geoffrey Brown, General Synod staff, London

Mr. Phill Butler, InterDev, Seattle

Mr. Bruce Cannon, Director of Board of Communication, Church of Scotland

Rev. Duncan Capewell, Religious Producer, Westsound

Rev. Heikki Castrén, former Director of Information, Church of Finland

Mons. Francesco Ceriotti, Italian Bishops' Conference

Don Tarcisio Cesarato, Order of St. Paul, Rome

Mr. Ross Coad, Templar Trust

Miss Margaret Coen, Link-Up Television

Mr. Philip Crookes, European Institute for the Media

Mrs. Ann Davies, Church of Scotland

Dr. Howard Davis, University of Kent

Mr. John Q. Davis, Christian Broadcasting Campaign

Mr. Jon Davey, Cable Authority, U.K.

Mr. Piet Derksen, Belgium

Drs. Bert P. Dorenbos, Rainbow Family Channel

Rev. Leslie Dorn SJ, *Niels Steensens Kollegium*, Copenhagen

M. Michel Evan, *Sofica Lumière*, Paris

Rev. Dr. Hans Florin, United Bible Societies, Europe and Middle East Region

The Most Rev. John P. Foley, President, Pontifical Council for Social Communications, Rome

Rev. Professor Duncan Forrester, University of Edinburgh

Mrs. Kirsten Fougner, Church of Norway

Dr. Ivo Fürer, Council of European Catholic Bishops' Conferences

Rev. John Geaney, Catholic VISN Producers, Washington DC

Professor Roberto Giannatelli, Salesian University, Rome

Mr. Gunnar Grøndahl, NRK

Mr. Robin Gurney, Council of European Churches, Geneva

Mr. Christer Hedin, Swedish Radio

Mr. Terje Hergetun, Pentecostal Church, Oslo

Herr Hans-Wolfgang Hessler, German Evangelical Church, Frankfurt

Rev. Albert van den Heuvel, NOS

Rev. Norman Hjelm, Lutheran World Federation, Geneva

The Right Rev. Crispian Hollis, Bishop of Portsmouth

Rev. David Holloway, Vicar of Jesmond

The Home Office, London

Rev. Peter Hyson, Pilgrim Radio

Mr. Ove Ingvaldstad, *Danvik folkehøyskole*, Drammen

The Right Rev. Colin James, Bishop of Winchester

Mr. Walter Kast, Agape Europe

Mr. John Kiis, Tallinn, Estonia and Roxboro, Quebec

Mr.Wim Koole, European Ecumenical Satellite Committee

Mr. Anders Lageson, *Kanalen TV*, Malmö

Dr. Rune Larsson, University of Lund

Mr. Anders Laugesen, Danmarks Radio

Rev. Dr. Lukáks László, Budapest

Mr. Magne Lerø, IMMI

Don Franco Lever, Salesian University

Mr. Birger Lind, KKR, Copenhagen

Dr. Ingmar Lindqvist, Church of Finland

Asst. Professor Knut Lundby, University of Oslo

Dr. Georg-Michael Luyken, Munich

Dr. Renato Maiocchi, Federation of Italian Protestant Churches

Rev. Christopher Martin, formerly IBA

Père Guy Martinot SJ, Louvain-la-Neuve, Belgium

Rev. Willy McDade, Director of Catholic Media Centre, Archdiocese of Glasgow

Dr. Jim McDonnell, Catholic Communications Centre, London

Sister Margaret McHard SND, Chesters College, Glasgow and Gillis College, Edinburgh

Père Gabriel Nissim, Le Jour de Seigneur, Paris

Mr. Fred Nyman, IBRA

Mr. Malachi O'Docherty, BBC Radio Ulster

Rev. Matti Paloheimo, Church of Finland

Mrs. Elmi Pata, Lutheran Church of Estonia

Rev. Professor Toomas Paul, Lutheran Church of Estonia

Professor Thorleif Pettersson, University of Uppsala

Dr. Charles Peterson, *Danvik folkehøyskole*, Drammen
Rev. Ian Phelps, Diocese of Leicester
Dr. Horst Pöttker, German Evangelical Church, Frankfurt
Mr. Tony Pragnell, formerly IBA
Rev. Robin Rees, European Religious Broadcasters Rádio Renascença, Lisbon
Rev. Edwin Robertson, formerly WACC
Dr. Jaakko Rusama, Church of Finland
Mr. Alan Sapper, ACTT, London
Mr. Richard Schoonhoven, KRO
Fraülein Murri Selle, German Evangelical Church, Munich
Rev. Eric Shegog, IBA
Mr. Michael Shoesmith, *Skopos*
Mr. Connie Sjoeberg, Lutheran World Federation, Geneva
Pastor Louis Simonfalvi, Budapest
SLOC, Cuijk, Netherlands
Mr. Roger H. Stanway, European Religious Broadcasters
Mrs. Karin Stigbrand, *Kabelnämden*, Stockholm
Mr. Stig Svärd, Stockholm
The Rt. Rev. John Taylor, Bishop of St. Albans
Mr. Bill Thatcher, ICMC, Seattle
Rev. Bert Tosh, BBC Radio Ulster
Dr. Bob Towler, Channel 4, London
Rev. Carlos Valle, WACC
Miss Rachel Viney, IBA
Bishop Bengt Wadensjø, Bishop of Karlstad
Mr. Charlie Warmington, BBC Radio Ulster
Professor George Wedell, European Institute for the Media
Mr. Nils-Gøran Wetterberg, Church of Sweden

Rev. John Wijngaards, Housetop, London
Mrs. Fran Wildish, Vision Broadcasting
Rev. Robert A. White SJ, Gregorian University, Rome
Miss Tiinakaisa Wikki, Church of Finland
Rev. Dr. Kenneth Wolfe, University of Kent

Twenty-seven Diocesan Communications Officers of the Church of England who kindly took part in a postal survey of communication needs.

Many of the participants at the following international gatherings in 1990:

European Catholic Bishops' Committee for the Media, Fatima, Portugal

RCC 90 (Religious Communications Conference), Nashville, Tennessee, USA

ERB (European Religious Broadcasters), Doncaster, England

The renaming of the *Institut de Journalisme*/European Media Studies as the Robert Schuman Institute, Brussels, Belgium

THE AUTHOR

Canon Peter Elvy has written a great deal on communication subjects and he has made a special study of the North American Electronic Church. He has wide experience in broadcasting. He is married with three children and has been vicar of an Essex parish since 1975. For the last ten years he has also been the Bishop of Chelmsford's Projects Officer. Peter Elvy is editor of the ecumenical quarterly *The Sower*.